THE FOLGER LIBRARY SHAKESPEARE

Designed to make Shakespeare's classic plays available to the general reader, each edition contains a reliable text with modernized spelling and punctuation, scene-by-scene plot summaries, and explanatory notes clarifying obscure and obsolete expressions. An interpretive essay and accounts of Shakespeare's life and theater form an instructive preface to each play.

Louis B. Wright, General Editor, was the Director of the Folger Shakespeare Library from 1948 until his retirement in 1968. He is the author of *Middle-Class Culture in Elizabethan England, Religion and Empire, Shakespeare for Everyman,* and many other books and essays on the history and literature of the Tudor and Stuart periods.

Virginia Lamar, Assistant Editor, served as research assistant to the Director and Executive Secretary of the Folger Shakespeare Library from 1946 until her death in 1968. She is the author of *English Dress in the Age of Shakespeare* and *Travel and Roads in England,* and coeditor of William Strachey's *Historie of Travell into Virginia Britania.*

The Folger Shakespeare Library

The Folger Shakespeare Library in Washington, D.C., a research institute founded and endowed by Henry Clay Folger and administered by the Trustees of Amherst College, contains the world's largest collection of Shakespeareana. Although the Folger Library's primary purpose is to encourage advanced research in history and literature, it has continually exhibited a profound concern in stimulating a popular interest in the Elizabethan period.

A complete brochure of the materials produced under the guidance of Louis B. Wright and Virginia A. LaMar—texts of the plays, supplementary reading, and recordings—is available free on request from Washington Square Press, a Simon & Schuster division of Gulf & Western Corporation, Educational Department, 1230 Avenue of the Americas, New York, N.Y. 10020.

GENERAL EDITOR

LOUIS B. WRIGHT

Director, Folger Shakespeare Library, 1948–1968

ASSISTANT EDITOR

VIRGINIA A. LaMAR

Executive Secretary, Folger Shakespeare Library, 1946–1968

The Folger Library General Reader's Shakespeare

ANTONY
AND
CLEOPATRA

WILLIAM
SHAKESPEARE

PUBLISHED BY POCKET BOOKS NEW YORK

POCKET BOOKS, a Simon & Schuster division of
GULF & WESTERN CORPORATION
1230 Avenue of the Americas, New York, N.Y. 10020

ISBN: 0-671-48938-0

First Pocket Books printing November, 1961

20 19 18 17 16 15 14 13

Printed in the U.S.A.

Preface

This edition of *Antony and Cleopatra* is designed to make available a readable text of one of Shakespeare's most popular plays. In the centuries since Shakespeare many changes have occurred in the meanings of words, and some clarification of Shakespeare's vocabulary may be helpful. To provide the reader with necessary notes in the most accessible format, we have placed them on the pages facing the text that they explain. We have tried to make these notes as brief and simple as possible. Preliminary to the text we have also included a brief statement of essential information about Shakespeare and his stage. Readers desiring more detailed information should refer to the books suggested in the references, and if still further information is needed, the bibliographies in those books will provide necessary clues to the literature of the subject.

The early texts of all of Shakespeare's plays provide only inadequate stage directions, and it is conventional for modern editors to add many that clarify the action. Such additions, and additions to entrances, are placed in square brackets.

All illustrations are from material in the Folger Library collections.

L. B. W.
V. A. L.

March 1, 1961

Egyptian Enchantress

In *Antony and Cleopatra* Shakespeare turned to a theme that had long fascinated the world and would continue to excite interest for centuries to come. Long before Shakespeare, Englishmen had available an account of Cleopatra and her lover Antony in Geoffrey Chaucer's *Legend of Good Women*, an odd place for an enchantress like the Egyptian queen to appear, but Chaucer conveniently forgot a portion of her history to reveal her as an example of faithful love. Later writers retold the story with varying interpretations until Cleopatra was as familiar to Englishmen as the most popular folk heroine of their own country. Before Shakespeare put the famous lovers into a drama these characters had already enjoyed a stage life. Samuel Daniel composed a *Tragedy of Cleopatra* (1594), which he revised in 1607, adding some characters apparently suggested by Shakespeare's play. *Antony and Cleopatra* probably dates from early in 1607, though Sir Edmund Chambers and others suggest that it might have appeared on the stage sometime in 1606.

Other dramatists also found the theme of Cleopatra's love a congenial subject. Samuel Brandon, about whom little is known, wrote a play which shifted the emphasis somewhat and gave it the title of *The Virtuous Octavia* (1594–1598). Mary Herbert,

Countess of Pembroke, translated from the French Robert Garnier's *Marc-Antoine,* which she published under the title of *Antony* (1592). Fulke Greville, Lord Brooke, wrote a play of *Antony and Cleopatra* which is lost because he burned the manuscript in the year of Queen Elizabeth's death (1603).

The main source of information about Antony and Cleopatra for the Elizabethans was Plutarch. The story of Mark Antony's infatuation with the Egyptian Queen, as well as much detailed information about the events leading up to the denouement, was accessible to Shakespeare and his contemporaries in Thomas North's translation from the French version of Plutarch made by Jacques Amyot. The first edition of North, published in 1579, was immediately popular. It was not only a highly readable book but was also a ready reference work for Greek and Roman history. Henceforth dramatists in search of plots based on historical episodes in the ancient world had only to turn to Plutarch, where they could find not only facts but picturesque detail and colorful language. This work was the main source for Shakespeare's *Antony and Cleopatra,* though he may have found a few incidents and suggestions in other easily available classical works. He must have been aware of the earlier plays on the subject, particularly Daniel's, but his own work shows little or no indebtedness to his predecessors.

Hamlet, with 3,929 lines, is Shakespeare's longest play, but *Antony and Cleopatra* comes close behind with 3,059 lines. Neither play could possibly have been acted in an Elizabethan theatre without some cutting, even if we take into account the bare platform stage which required no waiting for scene-shifting. The problem of the vast number of scenes in *Antony and Cleopatra* has troubled modern critics and producers, but we must remember that the act-and-scene division familiar in modern texts was an innovation by the earliest editor, Nicholas Rowe; the First Folio gave only a hint of act-and-scene division by printing at the beginning "Act One, Scene One," omitting all references to any division after that. We must imagine *Antony and Cleopatra* as performed on the Elizabethan stage with rapid entrances and exits, and not as rendered in the nineteenth century with realistic scenery and changes to emphasize locality at the entrance of each new set of characters. The Elizabethans were not locality conscious. If the dialogue indicated Actium in one scene and Alexandria in the next, it was all one to the average spectator at the Globe. It was the action—the dramatic story—that counted.

The time covered in the play was also of little moment to audiences not yet concerned about the classical unities. Historically the narrative covers the ten years from Fulvia's death in 40 B.C. to Cleopatra's death on August 29, 30 B.C. On the stage, the action covers twelve days. Thus Shakespeare telescoped history for dramatic effect and produced a play that gave the illusion of compactness. The fact that incidents in the play actually spread over a decade went unnoticed by the spectators.

In *Antony and Cleopatra* Shakespeare put behind him idyllic love, which he had treated more than a dozen years before in *Romeo and Juliet,* and turned his attention to the consuming passion of two characters who had already run the gamut of human emotion. Six or seven years before, Shakespeare had portrayed Antony as the devoted friend of Julius Cæsar, the orator at his funeral, and the leader of the victorious faction that put to rout Cæsar's assassins. Now we see Antony, an older if not a wiser man, a leader who could still command the allegiance and loyalty of half the Roman world. This man, exuberant in all his emotions, great of soul and equally great in his vices, matches his wit, his courage, and his passion with the most cunning siren of the East, Cleopatra.

A lesser dramatist of the period might have made this play a struggle between the good and evil angels for the soul of Antony or of universal man, but Shakespeare in his own maturity chooses to treat a far subtler theme than the old morality-play motifs. With the detail of a clinical psychologist, he studies the impact upon one another of two complex characters, one a Roman and the other an Egyptian. In his hands, Antony and Cleopatra become not only the prototypes of man and woman but symbols of the Roman and Eastern worlds. Antony sums up in himself the good and the bad of Roman life; Cleopatra is the essence of the mystery of the East, an enchantress capable of exerting all the witchery associated in the Elizabethan mind with Egypt. Yet the tragic struggle in the play is not between Antony and Cleopatra, for Antony does not try to resist the serpent of the Nile. The struggle is rather in Antony's own soul as the Roman soldier at intervals remembers his duty in the face of the enervations of Eastern luxury and lust. In the end Antony's passion for Cleopatra completes his ruin, a ruin to which Shakespeare manages to give an air of grandeur.

Shakespeare does not concentrate attention upon the tragic hero as he does in *Macbeth, Hamlet, Othello,* and *Lear.* Indeed, Antony is not that kind of hero. The audience's interest is not in the cosmic quality of Antony's spiritual struggles, for Shakespeare does not emphasize any soul-searching that Antony may have done on the few occasions that he had leisure for his Roman soul. We are concerned rather with the ruin that overtakes a great soldier, one who had held a third part of the world, because he allows passionate lust to dominate his life and obliterate his sense of duty.

The interest of the spectator and the reader focuses upon Cleopatra as much as or more than upon Antony. Shakespeare changed the characterization that he found in Plutarch to make her the epitome of feminine sorcery rather than the wily sovereign bent upon maintaining the power of her dynasty. The dramatist was oblivious to the historical Cleopatra because he wanted to write a play of grand passion that required him to simplify Cleopatra's character and make her the sum of all passionate women. In the play, her thoughts are all of Antony and of love. Egypt can go to wrack and ruin if only she can spend ambrosial days and nights with her lover. This is distinctly not the Cleopatra of history who coolly poisoned one brother to keep him from sharing her throne and spent much of her energy and thought in the effort to outwit Roman conquerors and strengthen her own authority. In Shakespeare's treatment, Cleopatra is first and foremost a woman in love, a realistic woman who recognizes her status in the eyes of other women. She knows she is mistress rather than wife and voices her spite at those women who occupy more favored positions. Her contempt for the virtuous Octavia is unbounded and she hates the memory of dead Fulvia.

The characters who bustle through the scenes of this play of action are genuine human beings and not abstractions for virtues and vices. By giving to Cleopatra the foibles and frailties of ordinary mortals, Shakespeare made her vivid to his audiences. In like manner,

Antony is understandable because he is a human who makes small mistakes as well as great ones and is susceptible to emotions and reactions characteristic of individuals known to us all.

Although *Antony and Cleopatra* is primarily a drama of action, the portrayal and contrast of character add much to the richness of the play. Against the dashing, exuberant, willful, and indiscreet Antony, we see Octavius as a cold, calculating, and adroit politician-in-arms, one who only at rare intervals, as at the news of Antony's death, allows himself the luxury of a generous thought. Against Cleopatra we see Octavia, who, if not as icy as her brother, is nevertheless chilly and obviously correct in all her behavior. The lesser characters are also made vivid by realistic touches. Enobarbus, bluff and cynical in his outward demeanor, has a sentimental streak often characteristic of his kind, and we think of him as a living personality. Even the country yokel who brings the asps to Cleopatra, like many of Shakespeare's rural types, is drawn with accurate detail. Throughout the play, we are dealing with living beings, not with cardboard figures.

The poetry of Antony and Cleopatra has been highly praised by critics, particularly by those modern critics who see much compact meaning in many of the more difficult passages. Shakespeare clearly was writing with less lyrical abandon than he had shown earlier in *Richard II*, let us say, or in *Romeo and Juliet*. He had matured and his lines were now often packed with an intensity of both emotion and meaning. Occasionally lines are too cryptic or too filled with a diversity of ideas and metaphors. Magnificent as is much of the poetry, we sometimes wish with Ben Jonson that Shakespeare had taken the trouble to blot a few lines. The play, evidently written with speed and intensity, contains passages that would have benefited from revision and judicious cutting. Perhaps the author knew that something would have to be cut, as he must have intended for *Hamlet* to be cut. Much nonsense has been uttered about the sacredness of Shakespeare's text. As a practical man of the theatre, he realized that no two performances are ever identical and that in acting much adaptation may be required. So he wrote *in extenso* as ideas and words crowded upon him, conscious that he or some of his theatrical colleagues would adapt the play to the time and spatial requirements of the stage.

The modern reader of *Antony and Cleopatra* should remember one fact about Elizabethan stage conditions, and that is the absence of women performers. On Shakespeare's stage, *Cleopatra* was acted by a boy, and that determined the quality of the love scenes. In these Shakespeare shows extraordinary skill in the power of suggestion through words rather than action. Where Hollywood would insert torrid bedroom scenes just barely decent enough to escape the censor, Shakespeare supplies poetry; metaphor and suggestion take the place of visual love-making which would have been distasteful. Rarely are Antony and Cleopatra shown together on the stage in scenes of passionate affection. When on one occasion they embrace, it is a very perfunctory sort of action. We hear much about Cleopatra's physical charms but we see little of them in the flesh. Shakespeare was a careful and sensible playwright who knew how to adapt his subject matter to the limitations of his stage. When Hollywood completes its latest version on the theme of these immortal lovers it will be nothing like Shakespeare's.

STAGE HISTORY

Of the productions of *Antony and Cleopatra* in Shakespeare's own time we have no records. No contemporary references allude to its success or failure. It was undoubtedly designed for the Globe, but what its reception was we do not know. All we know is that the theme was a popular one in contemporary literature and the play had the elements to make it a success. That it had a favorable reception may be suggested by the fact that it was selected for production by the King's Company after the reopening of the theatres at the Restoration in 1660, though there is no record of its performance by this company. Shakespeare's play was eclipsed by Sir Charles Sedley's *Antony and Cleopatra* in 1677 and by Dryden's play *All for Love, or, The World Well Lost* in 1678.

Dryden announced that his own version of the dramatic story was "Written in Imitation of Shakespeare's Stile." Since Dryden made his drama a love-and-honor tragedy in the style then fashionable, it was an instant success, and indeed it remained a popular piece in the theatre for generations. Dryden held the stage until David Garrick revived Shakespeare's version in 1759, but not even Garrick could drive Dryden's play from the theatre. Actually, Dryden's play, with its unified action and its concentration upon the unities of time and place, made it an easier play to stage and to comprehend.

John Philip Kemble sought to succeed with a version in 1813 which combined Dryden and Shakespeare in what the motion-picture industry today would call a "spectacular," complete with sensational scenic effects and music. Nineteenth- and early twentieth-century versions of Shakespeare's *Antony and Cleopatra* continued to emphasize spectacular scenery and elaborate productions that tried to provide visions of Oriental luxury, with a voluptuous siren in the role of Cleopatra.

But on neither side of the Atlantic was this play consistently successful. After a performance in New York on April 2, 1859, in which Madame Ponisi took the part of Cleopatra, the New York *Herald* commented of this overly plump siren that she was "not quite fascinating enough to make one throw away an empire." Nevertheless, the role of Cleopatra has frequently been an allurement to actresses, sometimes to their discomfiture. Tallulah Bankhead tried it in New York in the season of 1937–1938, but the play lasted only five performances. Katherine Cornell played the role in 1947–1948 with somewhat greater success. Despite its difficulty and its record of frequent failures, the play was seen at intervals throughout the nineteenth century and has been rather frequently revived in the twentieth. Perhaps its scope is too large for the modern stage. Professor Hazelton Spencer comments that "Of all Shakespeare's dramas this is the one in direst need of transposition to the motion-picture screen."

THE TEXT

The earliest text of *Antony and Cleopatra* is that printed in the First Folio of 1623. It was entered in the Stationers' Register on May 20, 1608, but no quarto version of the play is known to have been printed. The text of the First Folio shows a considerable number of misprints, many mislineations, and some eccentric punctuation. The present editors have made the corrections that seemed obviously required and accepted a number of emendations suggested by earlier textual critics.

THE AUTHOR

As early as 1598 Shakespeare was so well known as a literary and dramatic craftsman that Francis Meres, in his *Palladis Tamia: Wits Treasury,* referred in flattering terms to him as "mellifluous and honey-tongued Shakespeare," famous for his *Venus and Adonis,* his *Lucrece,* and "his sugared sonnets," which were circulating "among his private friends." Meres observes further that "as Plautus and Seneca are accounted the best for comedy and tragedy among the Latins, so Shakespeare among the English is the most excellent in both kinds for the stage," and he mentions a dozen plays that had made a name for Shakespeare. He concludes with the remark "that the Muses would speak with Shakespeare's fine filed phrase if they would speak English."

To those acquainted with the history of the Elizabethan and Jacobean periods, it is incredible that anyone should be so naïve or ignorant as to doubt the reality of Shakespeare as the author of the plays that bear his name. Yet so much nonsense has been written about other "candidates" for the plays that it is well to remind readers that no credible evidence that would stand up in a court of law has ever been adduced to prove either that Shakespeare did not write his plays or that anyone else wrote them. All the theories offered for the authorship of Francis Bacon, the Earl of Derby, the Earl of Oxford, the Earl of Hertford, Christopher Marlowe, and a score of other candidates are mere conjectures spun from the active imaginations of persons who confuse hypothesis and conjecture with evidence.

As Meres' statement of 1598 indicates, Shakespeare was already a popular playwright whose name carried weight at the box office. The obvious reputation of Shakespeare as early as 1598 makes the effort to prove him a myth one of the most absurd in the history of human perversity.

The anti-Shakespeareans talk darkly about a plot of vested interests to maintain the authorship of Shakespeare. Nobody has any vested interest in Shakespeare, but every scholar is interested in the truth and in the quality of evidence advanced by special pleaders who set forth hypotheses in place of facts.

The anti-Shakespeareans base their arguments upon a few simple premises, all of them false. These false premises are that Shakespeare was an unlettered yokel without any schooling, that nothing is known about Shakespeare, and that only a noble lord or the equivalent in background could have written the plays. The facts are that more is known about Shakespeare than about most dramatists of his day, that he had a very good education, acquired in the Stratford Grammar School, that the plays show no evidence of profound book learning, and that the knowledge of kings and courts evident in the plays is no greater than any intelligent young man could have picked up at second hand. Most anti-Shakespeareans are naïve and betray an obvious snobbery. The author of their favorite plays, they imply, must have had a college diploma framed and hung on his study wall like the one in their dentist's office, and obviously so great a writer must have had a title or some equally significant evidence of exalted social background. They forget that genius has a way of cropping up in unexpected places and that none of the great creative writers of the world got his inspiration in a college or university course.

William Shakespeare was the son of John Shakespeare of Stratford-upon-Avon, a substantial citizen of that small but busy market town in the center of the rich agricultural county of Warwick. John Shakespeare kept a shop, what we would call a general store; he dealt in wool and other produce and gradually acquired property. As a youth, John Shakespeare had learned the trade of glover and leather worker. There is no contemporary evidence that the elder Shakespeare was a butcher, though the anti-Shakespeareans like to talk about the ignorant "butcher's boy of Stratford." Their only evidence is a statement by gossipy John Aubrey, more than a century after William Shakespeare's birth, that young William followed his father's trade, and when he killed a calf, "he would do it in a high style and make a speech." We would like to believe the story true, but Aubrey is not a very credible witness.

John Shakespeare probably continued to operate a farm at Snitterfield that his father had leased. He married Mary Arden, daughter of his father's landlord, a man of some property. The third of their eight children was William, baptized on April 26, 1564, and probably born three days before. At least, it is conventional to celebrate April 23 as his birthday.

The Stratford records give considerable information about John Shakespeare. We know that he held several municipal offices including those of alderman and mayor. In 1580 he was in some sort of legal difficulty and was fined for neglecting a summons of the Court of Queen's Bench requiring him to appear at Westminster and be bound over to keep the peace.

As a citizen and alderman of Stratford, John Shakespeare was entitled to send his son to the grammar school free. Though the records are lost, there can be no reason to doubt that this is where young William received his education. As any student of the period knows, the grammar schools provided the basic education in Latin learning and literature. The Elizabethan grammar school is not to be confused with modern grammar schools. Many cultivated men of the day received all their formal education in the grammar schools. At the universities in this period a student would have received little training that would have inspired him to be a creative writer. At Stratford young Shakespeare would have acquired a familiarity with Latin and some little knowledge of Greek. He would have read Latin authors and become acquainted with the plays of Plautus and Terence. Undoubtedly, in this period of his life he received that stimulation to read and explore for himself the world of ancient and modern history which he later utilized in his plays. The youngster who does not acquire this type of intellectual curiosity *before* college days rarely develops as a result of a college course the kind of mind Shakespeare demonstrated. His learning in books was anything but profound, but he clearly had the probing curiosity that sent him in search of information, and he had a keenness in the observation of nature and of humankind that finds reflection in his poetry.

There is little documentation for Shakespeare's boyhood. There is little reason why there should be. Nobody knew that he was going to be a dramatist about whom any scrap of information would be prized in the centuries to come. He was merely an active and vigorous youth of Stratford, perhaps assisting his father in his business, and no Boswell bothered to write down facts about him. The most important record that we have is a marriage license issued by the Bishop of Worcester on November 28, 1582, to permit William Shakespeare to marry Anne Hathaway, seven or eight years his senior; furthermore, the Bishop permitted the marriage after reading the banns only once instead of three times, evidence of the desire for haste. The need was explained on May 26, 1583, when the christening of Susanna, daughter of William and Anne Shakespeare, was recorded at Stratford. Two years later, on February 2, 1585, the records show the birth of twins to the Shakespeares, a boy and a girl who were christened Hamnet and Judith.

What William Shakespeare was doing in Stratford during the early years of his married life, or when he went to London, we do not know. It has been conjectured that he tried his hand at schoolteaching, but that is a mere guess. There is a legend that he left Stratford to escape a charge of poaching in the park of Sir Thomas Lucy of Charlecote, but there is no proof of this. There is also a legend that when first he came to London, he earned his living by holding horses outside a playhouse and presently was given employment inside, but there is nothing better than eighteenth-century hearsay for this. How Shakespeare broke into the London theatres as a dramatist and actor we do not know. But lack of information is not surprising, for Elizabethans did not write their autobiographies, and we know even less about the lives of many writers and some men of affairs than we know about Shakespeare. By 1592 he was so well established and popular that he incurred the envy of the dramatist and pamphleteer Robert Greene, who referred to him as an "upstart crow . . . in his own conceit the only Shake-scene in a country." From this time onward, contemporary allusions and references in legal documents enable the scholar to chart Shakespeare's career with greater accuracy than is possible with most other Elizabethan dramatists.

By 1594 Shakespeare was a member of the company of actors known as the Lord Chamberlain's Men. After the accession of James I, in 1603, the company would have the sovereign for their patron and would be known as the King's Men. During the period of its greatest prosperity, this company would have as its principal theatres the Globe and the Blackfriars. Shakespeare was both an actor and a shareholder in the company. Tradition has assigned him such acting roles as Adam in *As You Like It* and the Ghost in *Hamlet*, a modest place on the stage that suggests that he may have had other duties in the management of the company. Such conclusions, however, are based on surmise.

What we do know is that his plays were popular and that he was highly successful in his vocation. His first play may have been *The Comedy of Errors*, acted perhaps in 1591. Certainly this was one of his earliest plays. The three parts of *Henry VI* were acted sometime between 1590 and 1592. Critics are not in agreement about precisely how much Shakespeare wrote of these three plays. *Richard III* probably dates from 1593. From this time onward, Shakespeare's plays followed on the stage in rapid succession: *Titus Andronicus, The Taming of the Shrew, The Two Gentlemen of Verona, Love's Labour's Lost, Romeo and Juliet, Richard II, A Midsummer Night's Dream, King John, The Merchant of Venice, Henry IV (Parts 1 and 2), Much Ado About Nothing, Henry V, Julius Cæsar, As You Like It, Twelfth Night, Hamlet, The Merry Wives of Windsor, All's Well That Ends Well,*

Measure for Measure, Othello, King Lear, and nine others that followed before Shakespeare retired completely, about 1613.

In the course of his career in London, he made enough money to enable him to retire to Stratford with a competence. His purchase on May 4, 1597, of New Place, then the second-largest dwelling in Stratford, a "pretty house of brick and timber," with a handsome garden, indicates his increasing prosperity. There his wife and children lived while he busied himself in the London theatres. The summer before he acquired New Place, his life was darkened by the death of his only son, Hamnet, a child of eleven. In May, 1602, Shakespeare purchased one hundred and seven acres of fertile farmland near Stratford and a few months later bought a cottage and garden across the alley from New Place. About 1611, he seems to have returned permanently to Stratford, for the next year a legal document refers to him as "William Shakespeare of Stratford-upon-Avon . . . gentleman." To achieve the desired appellation of gentleman, William Shakespeare had seen to it that the College of Heralds in 1596 granted his father a coat of arms. In one step he thus became a second-generation gentleman.

Shakespeare's daughter Susanna made a good match in 1607 with Dr. John Hall, a prominent and prosperous Stratford physician. His second daughter, Judith, did not marry until she was thirty-two years old, and then, under somewhat scandalous circumstances, she married Thomas Quiney, a Stratford vintner. On March 25, 1616, Shakespeare made his will, bequeathing his landed property to Susanna, £300 to Judith, certain sums to other relatives, and his second-best bed to his wife, Anne. Much has been made of the second-best bed, but the legacy probably indicates only that Anne liked that particular bed. Shakespeare, following the practice of the time, may have already arranged with Susanna for his wife's care. Finally, on April 23, 1616, the anniversary of his birth, William Shakespeare died, and he was buried on April 25 within the chancel of Trinity Church, as befitted an honored citizen. On August 6, 1623, a few months before the publication of the collected edition of Shakespeare's plays, Anne Shakespeare joined her husband in death.

THE PUBLICATION OF HIS PLAYS

During his lifetime Shakespeare made no effort to publish any of his plays, though eighteen appeared in print in single-play editions known as quartos. Some of these are corrupt versions known as "bad quartos." No quarto, so far as is known, had the author's approval. Plays were not considered "literature" any more than most radio and television scripts today are considered literature. Dramatists sold their plays outright to the theatrical companies and it was usually considered in the company's interest to keep plays from getting into print. To achieve a reputation as a man of letters, Shakespeare wrote his *Sonnets* and his narrative poems, *Venus and Adonis* and *The Rape of Lucrece*, but he probably never dreamed that his plays would establish his reputation as a literary genius. Only Ben Jonson, a man known for his colossal conceit, had the crust to call his plays *Works*, as he did when he published an edition in 1616. But men laughed at Ben Jonson.

After Shakespeare's death, two of his old colleagues in the King's Men, John Heminges and Henry Condell, decided that it would be a good thing to print, in more accurate versions than were then available, the plays already published and eighteen additional plays not previously published in quarto. In 1623 appeared *Mr. William Shakespeares Comedies, Histories, & Tragedies. Published according to the True Originall Copies. London. Printed by Isaac Iaggard and Ed. Blount.* This was the famous First Folio, a work that had the authority of Shakespeare's associates. The only play commonly attributed to Shakespeare that was omitted in the First Folio was *Pericles.* In their preface, "To the great Variety of Readers," Heminges and Condell state that whereas "you were abused with diverse stolen and surreptitious copies, maimed and deformed by the frauds and stealths of injurious impostors that exposed them, even those are now offered to your view cured and perfect of their limbs; and all the rest, absolute in their numbers, as he conceived them." What they used for printer's copy is one of the vexed problems of scholarship, and skilled bibliographers have devoted years of study to the question of the relation of the "copy" for the First Folio to Shakespeare's manuscripts. In some cases it is clear that the editors corrected printed quarto versions of the plays, probably by comparison with playhouse scripts. Whether these scripts were in Shakespeare's autograph is anybody's guess. No manuscript of any play in Shakespeare's handwriting has survived. Indeed, very few play manuscripts from this period by any author are extant. The Tudor and Stuart periods had not yet learned to prize autographs and authors' original manuscripts.

Since the First Folio contains eighteen plays not previously printed, it is the only source for these. For the other eighteen, which had appeared in quarto versions, the First Folio also has the authority of an edition prepared and overseen by Shakespeare's colleagues and professional associates. But since editorial standards in 1623 were far from strict, and Heminges and Condell were actors rather than editors by profession, the texts are sometimes careless. The printing and proofreading of the First Folio also left much to be desired, and some garbled passages have had to be corrected and emended. The "good quarto" texts have to be taken into account in preparing a modern edition.

Because of the great popularity of Shakespeare through the centuries, the First Folio has become a prized book, but it is not a very rare one, for it is estimated that 238 copies are extant. The Folger Shakespeare Library in Washington, D.C., has seventy-nine copies of the First Folio, collected by the founder, Henry Clay Folger, who believed that a collation of as many texts as possible would reveal significant facts about the text of Shakespeare's plays. Dr. Charlton Hinman, using an ingenious machine of his own invention for mechanical collating, has made many discoveries that throw light on Shakespeare's text and on printing practices of the day.

The probability is that the First Folio of 1623 had an edition of between 1,000 and 1,250 copies. It is believed that it sold for £1, which made it an expensive book, for £1 in 1623 was equivalent to something between $40 and $50 in modern purchasing power.

During the seventeenth century, Shakespeare was sufficiently popular to warrant three later editions in folio size, the Second Folio of 1632, the Third Folio of 1663–1664, and the Fourth Folio of 1685. The Third Folio added six other plays ascribed to Shakespeare, but these are apocryphal.

THE SHAKESPEAREAN THEATRE

The theatres in which Shakespeare's plays were performed were vastly different from those we know today. The stage was a platform that jutted out into the area now occupied by the first rows of seats on the main floor, what is called the "orchestra" in America and the "pit" in England. This platform had no curtain to come down at the ends of acts and scenes. And although simple stage properties were available, the Elizabethan theatre lacked both the machinery and the elaborate movable scenery of the modern theatre. In the rear of the platform stage was a curtained area that could be used as an inner room, a tomb, or any such scene that might be required. A balcony above this inner room, and perhaps balconies on the sides of the stage, could represent the upper deck of a ship, the entry to Juliet's room, or a prison window. A trap door in the stage provided an entrance for ghosts and devils from the nether regions, and a similar trap in the canopied structure over the stage, known as the "heavens," made it possible to let down angels on a rope. These primitive stage arrangements help to account for many elements in Elizabethan plays. For example, since there was no curtain, the dramatist frequently felt the necessity of writing into his play action to clear the stage at the ends of acts and scenes. The funeral march at the end of *Hamlet* is not there merely for atmosphere; Shakespeare had to get the corpses off the stage. The lack of scenery also freed the dramatist from undue concern about the exact location of his sets, and the physical relation of his various settings to each other did not have to be

Courtesy Folger Shakespeare Library

The Swan (39), the Bear Garden (38), and the Globe (37).
From Merian's View of London (1638)

worked out with the same precision as in the modern theatre.

Before London had buildings designed exclusively for theatrical entertainment, plays were given in inns and taverns. The characteristic inn of the period had an inner courtyard with rooms opening onto balconies overlooking the yard. Players could set up their temporary stages at one end of the yard and audiences could find seats on the balconies out of the weather. The poorer sort could stand or sit on the cobblestones in the yard, which was open to the sky. The first theatres followed this construction, and throughout the Elizabethan period the large public theatres had a yard in front of the stage open to the weather, with two or three tiers of covered balconies extending around the theatre. This physical structure again influenced the writing of plays. Because a dramatist wanted the actors to be heard, he frequently wrote into his play orations that could be delivered with declamatory effect. He also provided spectacle, buffoonery, and broad jests to keep the riotous groundlings in the yard entertained and quiet.

In another respect the Elizabethan theatre differed greatly from ours. It had no actresses. All women's roles were taken by boys, sometimes recruited from the boys' choirs of the London churches. Some of these youths acted their roles with great skill and the Elizabethans did not seem to be aware of any incongruity. The first actresses on the professional English stage appeared after the Restoration of Charles II, in 1660, when exiled Englishmen brought back from France practices of the French stage.

London in the Elizabethan period, as now, was the center of theatrical interest, though wandering actors from time to time traveled through the country performing in inns, halls, and the houses of the nobility. The first professional playhouse, called simply The Theatre, was erected by James Burbage, father of Shakespeare's colleague Richard Burbage, in 1576 on lands of the old Holywell Priory adjacent to Finsbury Fields, a playground and park area just north of the city walls. It had the advantage of being outside the city's jurisdiction and yet was near enough to be easily accessible. Soon after The Theatre was opened, another playhouse called The Curtain was erected in the same neighborhood. Both of these playhouses had open courtyards and were probably polygonal in shape.

About the time The Curtain opened, Richard Farrant, Master of the Children of the Chapel Royal at Windsor and of St. Paul's, conceived the idea of opening a "private" theatre in the old monastery buildings of the Blackfriars, not far from St. Paul's Cathedral in the heart of the city. This theatre was ostensibly to train the choirboys in plays for presentation at Court, but Farrant managed to present plays to paying audiences and achieved considerable success until aristocratic neighbors complained and had the theatre closed. This first Blackfriars Theatre was significant, however, because it popularized the boy actors in a professional way and it paved the way for a second theatre in the Blackfriars, which Shakespeare's company took over more than thirty years later. By the last years of the sixteenth century, London had at least six professional theatres and still others were erected during the reign of James I.

The Globe Theatre, the playhouse that most people connect with Shakespeare, was erected early in 1599 on the Bankside, the area across the Thames from the city. Its construction had a dramatic beginning, for on

The Globe Playhouse.
From Visscher's *View of London* (1616).

the night of December 28, 1598, James Burbage's sons, Cuthbert and Richard, gathered together a crew who tore down the old theatre in Holywell and carted the timbers across the river to a site that they had chosen for a new playhouse. The reason for this clandestine operation was a row with the landowner over the lease to the Holywell property. The site chosen for the Globe was another playground outside of the city's jurisdiction, a region of somewhat unsavory character. Not far away was the Bear Garden, an amphitheatre devoted to the baiting of bears and bulls. This was also the region occupied by many houses of ill fame licensed by the Bishop of Winchester and the source of substantial revenue to him. But it was easily accessible either from London Bridge or by means of the cheap boats operated by the London watermen, and it had the great advantage of being beyond the authority of the Puritanical aldermen of London, who frowned on plays because they lured apprentices from work, filled their heads with improper ideas, and generally exerted a bad influence. The aldermen also complained that the crowds drawn together in the theatre helped to spread the plague.

The Globe was the handsomest theatre up to its time. It was a large building, apparently octagonal in shape and open like its predecessors to the sky in the center, but capable of seating a large audience in its covered balconies. To erect and operate the Globe, the Burbages organized a syndicate composed of the leading members of the dramatic company, of which Shakespeare was a member. Since it was open to the weather and depended on natural light, plays had to be given in the afternoon. This caused no hardship in the long afternoons of an English summer, but in the winter the weather was a great handicap and discouraged all except the hardiest. For that reason, in 1608 Shakespeare's company was glad to take over the lease of the second Blackfriars Theatre, a substantial, roomy hall reconstructed within the framework of the old monastery building. This theatre was protected from the weather and its stage was artificially lighted by chandeliers of candles. This became the winter playhouse for Shakespeare's company and at once proved so popular that the congestion of traffic created an embarrassing problem. Stringent regulations had to be made for the movement of coaches in the vicinity. Shakespeare's company continued to use the Globe during the summer months. In 1613 a squib fired from a cannon during a performance of *Henry VIII* fell on the thatched roof and the Globe burned to the ground. The next year it was rebuilt.

London had other famous theatres. The Rose, just west of the Globe, was built by Philip Henslowe, a semiliterate denizen of the Bankside, who became one of the most important theatrical owners and producers of the Tudor and Stuart periods. What is more important for historians, he kept a detailed account book, which provides much of our information about theatrical history in his time. Another famous theatre on the Bankside was the Swan, which a Dutch priest, Johannes de Witt, visited in 1596. The crude drawing of the stage which he made was copied by his friend Arend van Buchell; it is one of the important pieces of contemporary evidence for theatrical construction. Among the other theatres, the Fortune, north of the city, on Golding Lane, and the Red Bull, even farther away from the city, off St. John's Street, were the most popular. The Red Bull, much frequented by apprentices, favored sensational and sometimes rowdy plays.

The actors who kept all of these theatres going were

Interior of the Swan Theatre.
From a drawing by Johannes de Witt (1596).

organized into companies under the protection of some noble patron. Traditionally actors had enjoyed a low reputation. In some of the ordinances they were classed as vagrants; in the phraseology of the time, "rogues, vagabonds, sturdy beggars, and common players" were all listed together as undesirables. To escape penalties often meted out to these characters, organized groups of actors managed to gain the protection of various personages of high degree. In the later years of Elizabeth's reign, a group flourished under the name of the Queen's Men; another group had the protection of the Lord Admiral and were known as the Lord Admiral's Men. Edward Alleyn, son-in-law of Philip Henslowe, was the leading spirit in the Lord Admiral's Men. Besides the adult companies, troupes of boy actors from time to time also enjoyed considerable popularity. Among these were the Children of Paul's and the Children of the Chapel Royal.

The company with which Shakespeare had a long association had for its first patron Henry Carey, Lord Hunsdon, the Lord Chamberlain, and hence they were known as the Lord Chamberlain's Men. After the accession of James I, they became the King's Men. This company was the great rival of the Lord Admiral's Men, managed by Henslowe and Alleyn.

All was not easy for the players in Shakespeare's time, for the aldermen of London were always eager for an excuse to close up the Blackfriars and any other theatres in their jurisdiction. The theatres outside the jurisdiction of London were not immune from interference, for they might be shut up by order of the Privy Council for meddling in politics or for various other offenses, or they might be closed in time of plague lest they spread infection. During plague times, the actors usually went on tour and played the provinces wherever they could find an audience. Particularly frightening were the plagues of 1592–1594 and 1613 when the theatres closed and the players, like many other Londoners, had to take to the country.

Though players had a low social status, they enjoyed great popularity, and one of the favorite forms of entertainment at Court was the performance of plays. To be commanded to perform at Court conferred great prestige upon a company of players, and printers frequently noted that fact when they published plays. Several of Shakespeare's plays were performed before the sovereign, and Shakespeare himself undoubtedly acted in some of these plays.

REFERENCES FOR FURTHER READING

Many readers will want suggestions for further reading about Shakespeare and his times. The literature in this field is enormous but a few references will serve as guides to further study. A simple and useful little book is Gerald Sanders, *A Shakespeare Primer* (New York, 1950). *A Companion to Shakespeare Studies,* edited by Harley Granville-Barker and G. B. Harrison (Cambridge, Eng., 1934) is a valuable guide. More detailed but still not too voluminous to be confusing is Hazelton Spencer, *The Art and Life of William Shakespeare* (New York, 1940) which, like Sanders' handbook, contains a brief annotated list of useful books on various aspects of the subject. The most detailed and scholarly work providing complete factual information about Shakespeare is Sir Edmund Chambers, *William Shakespeare: A Study of Facts and Problems* (2 vols.,

Oxford, 1930). For detailed, factual information about the Elizabethan and seventeenth-century stages, the definitive reference works are Sir Edmund Chambers, *The Elizabethan Stage* (4 vols., Oxford, 1923) and Gerald E. Bentley, *The Jacobean and Caroline Stage* (5 vols., Oxford, 1941–1956). Alfred Harbage, *Shakespeare's Audience* (New York, 1941) throws light on the nature and tastes of the customers for whom Elizabethan dramatists wrote.

Although specialists disagree about details of stage construction, the reader will find essential information in John C. Adams, *The Globe Playhouse: Its Design and Equipment* (Barnes & Noble, 1961). A model of the Globe playhouse by Dr. Adams is on permanent exhibition in the Folger Shakespeare Library in Washington, D.C. An excellent description of the architecture of the Globe is Irwin Smith, *Shakespeare's Globe Playhouse: A Modern Reconstruction in Text and Scale Drawings Based upon the Reconstruction of the Globe by John Cranford Adams* (New York, 1956). Another recent study of the physical characteristics of the Globe is C. Walter Hodges, *The Globe Restored* (London, 1953). An easily read history of the early theatres is J. Q. Adams, *Shakespearean Playhouses: A History of English Theatres from the Beginnings to the Restoration* (Boston, 1917).

The following titles on theatrical history will provide information about Shakespeare's plays in later periods: Alfred Harbage, *Theatre for Shakespeare* (Toronto, 1955); Esther Cloudman Dunn, *Shakespeare in America* (New York, 1939); George C. D. Odell, *Shakespeare from Betterton to Irving* (2 vols., London, 1921); Arthur Colby Sprague, *Shakespeare and the Actors: The Stage Business in His Plays (1660–1905)* (Cambridge, Mass., 1944) and *Shakespearian Players and Performances* (Cambridge, Mass., 1953); Leslie Hotson, *The Commonwealth and Restoration Stage* (Cambridge, Mass., 1928); Alwin Thaler, *Shakspere to Sheridan: A Book About the Theatre of Yesterday and To-day* (Cambridge, Mass., 1922); Ernest Bradlee Watson, *Sheridan to Robertson: A Study of the 19th-Century London Stage* (Cambridge, Mass., 1926). Enid Welsford, *The Court Masque* (Cambridge, Mass., 1927) is an excellent study of the characteristics of this form of entertainment.

Harley Granville-Barker, *Prefaces to Shakespeare* (5 vols., London, 1927–1948) provides stimulating critical discussion of the plays. An older classic of criticism is Andrew C. Bradley, *Shakespearean Tragedy: Lectures on Hamlet, Othello, King Lear, Macbeth* (London, 1904), which is now available in an inexpensive reprint (New York, 1955). Thomas M. Parrott, *Shakespearean Comedy* (New York, 1949) is scholarly and readable. Shakespeare's dramatizations of English history are examined in E. M. W. Tillyard, *Shakespeare's History Plays* (London, 1948), and Lily Bess Campbell, *Shakespeare's "Histories," Mirrors of Elizabethan Policy* (San Marino, Calif., 1947) contains a more technical discussion of the same subject.

The chapter on *Antony and Cleopatra* in Harley Granville-Barker, *Prefaces to Shakespeare* (London, 1958), I, 367–423, is useful and provocative, especially his sensible commentary on the acting of the play. M. W. MacCallum, *Shakespeare's Roman Plays and Their Background* (London, 1910) provides general information about Shakespeare's treatment of Roman history. The "Life of Antonius" in Sir Thomas North's Plutarch, *The Lives of the Noble Grecians and Romans* (1579) is available in various modern editions. C. F. Tucker Brooke edited a version of the sections used by

Shakespeare as *Shakespeare's Plutarch* (2 vols., London, 1909). Relevant sections in the *Cambridge Ancient History* (12 vols., Cambridge, Eng., 1923–1939) will provide information about the historical events covered in the play. The New Arden edition of *Antony and Cleopatra,* edited by M. R. Ridley (London, 1954) is useful for its commentary on recent scholarship, as is John Munro's edition in *The London Shakespeare* (6 vols., New York, 1958). A colorful essay on Cleopatra, giving the full story of her career, will be found in Ivor Brown, *Dark Ladies* (London, 1957).

The question of the authenticity of Shakespeare's plays arouses perennial attention. A book that demolishes the notion of hidden cryptograms in the plays is William F. Friedman and Elizebeth S. Friedman, *The Shakespearean Ciphers Examined* (New York, 1957). A succinct account of the various absurdities advanced to suggest the authorship of a multitude of candidates other than Shakespeare will be found in R. C. Churchill, *Shakespeare and His Betters* (Bloomington, Ind., 1959) and Frank W. Wadsworth, *The Poacher from Stratford: A Partial Account of the Controversy over the Authorship of Shakespeare's Plays* (Berkeley, Calif., 1958). An essay on the curious notions in the writings of the anti-Shakespeareans is that by Louis B. Wright, "The Anti-Shakespeare Industry and the Growth of Cults," *The Virginia Quarterly Review,* XXXV (1959), 289–303.

Interesting pictures as well as new information about Shakespeare will be found in F. E. Halliday, *Shakespeare, a Pictorial Biography* (London, 1956). Allardyce Nicoll, *The Elizabethans* (Cambridge, Eng., 1957) contains a variety of illustrations.

A brief, clear, and accurate account of Tudor history is S. T. Bindoff, *The Tudors,* in the Penguin series. A readable general history is G. M. Trevelyan, *The History of England,* first published in 1926 and available in many editions. G. M. Trevelyan, *English Social History,* first published in 1942 and also available in many editions, provides fascinating information about England in all periods. Sir John Neale, *Queen Elizabeth* (London, 1934) is the best study of the great Queen. Various aspects of life in the Elizabethan period are treated in Louis B. Wright, *Middle-Class Culture in Elizabethan England* (Chapel Hill, N.C., 1935; reprinted by Cornell University Press, 1958). *Shakespeare's England: An Account of the Life and Manners of His Age,* edited by Sidney Lee and C. T. Onions (2 vols., Oxford, 1916), provides a large amount of information on many aspects of life in the Elizabethan period. Additional information will be found in Muriel St. C. Byrne, *Elizabethan Life in Town and Country* (Barnes & Noble, 1961).

The Folger Shakespeare Library is currently publishing a series of illustrated pamphlets on various aspects of English life in the sixteenth and seventeenth centuries. The following titles are available: Dorothy E. Mason, *Music in Elizabethan England;* Craig R. Thompson, *The English Church in the Sixteenth Century;* Louis B. Wright, *Shakespeare's Theatre and the Dramatic Tradition;* Giles E. Dawson, *The Life of William Shakespeare;* Virginia A. LaMar, *English Dress in the Age of Shakespeare;* Craig R. Thompson, *The Bible in English, 1525–1611;* Craig R. Thompson, *Schools in Tudor England;* Craig R. Thompson, *Universities in Tudor England;* Lilly C. Stone, *English Sports and Recreations;* Conyers Read, *The Government of England under Elizabeth.* Virginia A. LaMar, *Travel and Roads in England.*

[*Dramatis Personae.*

Mark Antony, *Octavius Cæsar*, *M. Æmilius Lepidus*, Triumvirs.

Sextus Pompeius. *Domitius Enobarbus*, *Ventidius*, *Eros*, *Scarus*, *Dercetas*, *Demetrius*, *Philo*, friends to *Antony*.

Canidius, Lieutenant-General to *Antony*.

Mæcenas, *Agrippa*, *Dolabella*, *Proculeius*, *Thidias*, *Gallus*, friends to *Cæsar*.

Taurus, Lieutenant-General to *Cæsar*.

Menas, *Menecrates*, *Varrius*, friends to *Pompey*.

Silius, an Officer in the army of *Ventidius*.

Euphronius, an Ambassador from *Antony* to *Cæsar*.

Alexas, *Mardian*, *Seleucus*, *Diomedes*, attendants on *Cleopatra*.

A Soothsayer.

A Clown.

Cleopatra, Queen of Egypt.

Octavia, sister to *Cæsar* and later wife to *Antony*.

Charmian, *Iras*, ladies attending on *Cleopatra*.

Officers, Soldiers, Messengers, Attendants.

SCENE: *Several parts of the Roman Empire.*]

ANTONY AND CLEOPATRA

ACT I

I. Mark Antony, one of the triumvirs ruling the Roman empire, neglects his responsibilities and leads a scandalous life of sensual pleasure in Alexandria with Cleopatra, Queen of Egypt. He ignores messages from Octavius Cæsar and expresses irritation with news from Rome. Cleopatra uses every charm she possesses to alienate Antony from Rome and keep him in Alexandria, but inevitably civil disturbances call him away. The son of Pompey the Great is in revolt and Antony feels that action is required of him. Cleopatra taxes him with insincerity but in the end bids him a gracious farewell.

I. i. 3. **files and musters of the war:** troops drawn up in battle order.

4. **plated Mars:** the god of war, armored for battle; **bend:** incline their gaze, with implication of descent of attention to a less worthy object.

5. **The office and devotion of their view:** i.e., his full attention; **office** means function.

6. **tawny front:** swarthy forehead (face). Cleopatra, although of pure Greek blood, was pictured by Elizabethan Englishmen as dark-skinned.

8. **reneges all temper:** completely renounces its usual character.

10. **gypsy's:** The word **gypsy** derives from Egyptian, because of the belief that Egypt was the original home of the gypsies. In calling Cleopatra a gypsy, Philo expresses his contempt. Elizabethans regarded gypsies as highly undesirable characters.

13. **triple pillar:** one of the three pillars; i.e., one member of the triumvirate, the other two being Octavius Cæsar and Lepidus.

ACT I

Scene I. [Alexandria. A room in Cleopatra's Palace.]

Enter Demetrius and Philo.

Philo. Nay, but this dotage of our general's
O'erflows the measure. Those his goodly eyes
That o'er the files and musters of the war
Have glowed like plated Mars, now bend, now turn
The office and devotion of their view
Upon a tawny front. His captain's heart,
Which in the scuffles of great fights hath burst
The buckles on his breast, reneges all temper,
And is become the bellows and the fan
To cool a gypsy's lust.

Flourish. Enter Antony, Cleopatra, her Ladies, the Train, with Eunuchs fanning her.

Look where they come!
Take but good note, and you shall see in him
The triple pillar of the world transformed
Into a strumpet's fool. Behold and see.
Cleo. If it be love indeed, tell me how much.

18. **bourn:** limit.

22. **Grates me! The sum:** irritates me. Sum it up for me.

23. **them:** the news (Latin *res novae*), often a plural in Elizabethan English.

25. **scarce-bearded:** youthful.

28. **damn:** condemn.

30. **like:** likely.

31. **dismission:** dismissal.

33. **process:** summons.

36. **homager:** slave. "You blush," says Cleopatra, "because my accusation that Cæsar is your master is only too accurate"; **Else:** otherwise.

38-9. **the wide arch/Of the ranged empire:** the keystone of the wide-ranging empire.

"Plated" Mars—Guillaume Du Choul, ***Discours de la religion des anciens Romains*** **(1556) (See 1. 1. 4.)**

Ant. There's beggary in the love that can be reckoned.
Cleo. I'll set a bourn how far to be beloved.
Ant. Then must thou needs find out new heaven, new earth.

Enter a Messenger.

Mess. News, my good lord, from Rome.
Ant. Grates me! The sum.
Cleo. Nay, hear them, Antony.
Fulvia perchance is angry; or who knows
If the scarce-bearded Cæsar have not sent
His pow'rful mandate to you: Do this, or this;
Take in that kingdom, and enfranchise that;
Perform't, or else we damn thee.
Ant. How, my love?
Cleo. Perchance? Nay, and most like:
You must not stay here longer; your dismission
Is come from Cæsar; therefore hear it, Antony.
Where's Fulvia's process? Cæsar's I would say. Both?
Call in the messengers. As I am Egypt's Queen,
Thou blushest, Antony, and that blood of thine
Is Cæsar's homager! Else so thy cheek pays shame
When shrill-tongued Fulvia scolds. The messengers!
Ant. Let Rome in Tiber melt and the wide arch
Of the ranged empire fall! Here is my space.
Kingdoms are clay; our dungy earth alike
Feeds beast as man. The nobleness of life
Is to do thus [*Embracing her*] when such a mutual pair

44-6. **in which I bind,/. . . the world to weet/ We stand up peerless:** I challenge the world to admit that we have no equals as lovers. **Weet** means know, hence acknowledge.

47. **Excellent:** more than ordinary, excessive.

49-50. **I'll seem the fool I am not. Antony/Will be himself:** I'll pretend to be taken in by your false vows. Antony will always behave as he wishes.

51. **But stirred by Cleopatra:** unmoved by any influence except that of Cleopatra.

53. **confound:** waste, lose.

59. **passion:** strong emotion.

61. **No messenger but thine:** that is, I care only for news of you.

67-8. **that great property/Which still should go with Antony:** that greatness which should always characterize Antony.

70. **approves:** proves, confirms; **the common liar:** i.e., Rumor.

72. **Rest you happy:** may you keep fortunate, good-by.

And such a twain can do't, in which I bind,
On pain of punishment, the world to weet
We stand up peerless.

Cleo. Excellent falsehood!
Why did he marry Fulvia, and not love her?
I'll seem the fool I am not. Antony
Will be himself.

Ant. But stirred by Cleopatra.
Now for the love of Love and her soft hours,
Let's not confound the time with conference harsh.
There's not a minute of our lives should stretch
Without some pleasure now. What sport tonight?

Cleo. Hear the ambassadors.

Ant. Fie, wrangling queen!
Whom every thing becomes—to chide, to laugh,
To weep; whose every passion fully strives
To make itself, in thee, fair and admired!
No messenger but thine, and all alone
Tonight we'll wander through the streets and note
The qualities of people. Come, my queen;
Last night you did desire it.—Speak not to us.

Exeunt [Antony and Cleopatra] with the Train.

Dem. Is Cæsar with Antonius prized so slight?

Philo. Sir, sometimes when he is not Antony
He comes too short of that great property
Which still should go with Antony.

Dem. I am full sorry
That he approves the common liar, who
Thus speaks of him at Rome; but I will hope
Of better deeds tomorrow. Rest you happy!

Exeunt.

I. [ii.] 2. absolute: perfect.

4. charge: load. This is Lewis Theobald's emendation of the Folio reading "change." Charmian apparently refers to a taunt by Alexas that she will frequently betray her husband and that he will have to disguise in some fashion the horns which Elizabethans attributed to cuckolds. As G. L. Kittredge suggested, there is probably an allusion to the garlanded horns of sacrificial bulls.

19. in flesh: i.e., she will have more flesh on her body.

22. his prescience: i.e., "his learned Highness."

Bull decorated for sacrifice—Guillaume Du Choul, *Discours de la religion des anciens Romains* (1556)

[Scene II. Alexandria. Another room in Cleopatra's Palace.]

Enter a Soothsayer, Charmian, Iras, and Alexas.

Char. Lord Alexas, sweet Alexas, most anything Alexas, almost most absolute Alexas, where's the soothsayer that you praised so to the Queen? O that I knew this husband which, you say, must charge his horns with garlands!

Alex. Soothsayer!

Sooth. Your will?

Char. Is this the man? Is't you, sir, that know things?

Sooth. In nature's infinite book of secrecy
A little I can read.

Alex. Show him your hand.

[*Enter Enobarbus.*]

Eno. Bring in the banquet quickly; wine enough Cleopatra's health to drink.

Char. Good sir, give me good fortune.

Sooth. I make not, but foresee.

Char. Pray then, foresee me one.

Sooth. You shall be yet far fairer than you are.

Char. He means in flesh.

Iras. No, you shall paint when you are old.

Char. Wrinkles forbid!

Alex. Vex not his prescience; be attentive.

Char. Hush!

25. **with drinking:** instead of with love. The liver was believed to be the seat of passion.

27. **Good now:** if you will be so good, tell me now.

30. **me:** (the ethical dative). "Find for me that I shall marry."

34. **proved:** known by experience.

37. **belike:** probably.

41. **fertile:** Theobald's reading. The Folio reads "foretell."

42. **forgive thee for a witch:** clear you of any charge of sorcery.

43. **are privy to:** are in the secret of.

54. **an oily palm:** a hot, moist hand was supposed to indicate an amorous disposition. Cf. *Othello*, III. iv. 39, 41-3: "This hand is moist, my lady. . . . This argues fruitfulness and liberal heart./Hot, hot, and moist. This hand of yours requires/A sequester from liberty, fasting, and prayer. . . ."

Sooth. You shall be more beloving than beloved.

Char. I had rather heat my liver with drinking.

Alex. Nay, hear him.

Char. Good now, some excellent fortune! Let me be married to three kings in a forenoon and widow them all. Let me have a child at fifty, to whom Herod of Jewry may do homage. Find me to marry me with Octavius Cæsar, and companion me with my mistress.

Sooth. You shall outlive the lady whom you serve.

Char. O excellent! I love long life better than figs.

Sooth. You have seen and proved a fairer former fortune
Than that which is to approach.

Char. Then belike my children shall have no names. Prithee, how many boys and wenches must I have?

Sooth. If every of your wishes had a womb,
And fertile every wish, a million.

Char. Out, fool! I forgive thee for a witch.

Alex. You think none but your sheets are privy to your wishes.

Char. Nay, come, tell Iras hers.

Alex. We'll know all our fortunes.

Eno. Mine, and most of our fortunes, tonight, shall be—drunk to bed.

Iras. There's a palm presages chastity, if nothing else.

Char. E'en as the o'erflowing Nilus presageth famine.

Iras. Go, you wild bedfellow, you cannot soothsay.

Char. Nay, if an oily palm be not a fruitful prog-

56. **workyday:** everyday, ordinary.

66. **go:** probably both "walk" and "bear children" are intended; **Isis:** one of the chief goddesses of the Egyptian pantheon, their equivalent of a moon goddess.

72-3. **prayer of the people:** i.e., something everyone joins in asking.

75. **foul knave:** ugly rogue.

76. **keep decorum:** act appropriately.

nostication, I cannot scratch mine ear. Prithee tell her but a workyday fortune.

Sooth. Your fortunes are alike.

Iras. But how, but how? Give me particulars.

Sooth. I have said.

Iras. Am I not an inch of fortune better than she?

Char. Well, if you were but an inch of fortune better than I, where would you choose it?

Iras. Not in my husband's nose.

Char. Our worser thoughts heavens mend! Alexas —come, his fortune, his fortune! O, let him marry a woman that cannot go, sweet Isis, I beseech thee! and let her die too, and give him a worse! and let worse follow worse till the worst of all follow him laughing to his grave, fiftyfold a cuckold! Good Isis, hear me this prayer, though thou deny me a matter of more weight; good Isis, I beseech thee!

Iras. Amen. Dear goddess, hear that prayer of the people! For, as it is a heartbreaking to see a handsome man loose-wived, so it is a deadly sorrow to behold a foul knave uncuckolded. Therefore, dear Isis, keep decorum, and fortune him accordingly!

Char. Amen.

Alex. Lo now, if it lay in their hands to make me a cuckold, they would make themselves whores but they'ld do't!

Eno. Hush! Here comes Antony.

Enter Cleopatra.

Char. Not he! the Queen.

Cleo. Saw you my lord?

88. **A Roman thought:** i.e., a recollection of duty, perhaps inspired by news from Rome.

97. **the time's state:** the state of the times.

100. **better issue:** greater success.

103. **infects the teller:** makes the bearer appear as baneful as his news.

107. **as:** as if.

109. **Parthian force:** Parthia was a kingdom southeast of the Caspian Sea, inhabited by warlike people of Iranian stock.

110. **Extended:** forcibly seized, a legal sense of the word.

Mark Antony–Jacobus de Strada, *Epitome thesauri antiquitatum* (1557)

Eno. No, lady.
Cleo. Was he not here?
Char. No, madam.
Cleo. He was disposed to mirth; but on the sudden
A Roman thought hath struck him. Enobarbus!
Eno. Madam?
Cleo. Seek him, and bring him hither. Where's Alexas?
Alex. Here at your service. My lord approaches.

Enter Antony with a Messenger [and Attendants].

Cleo. We will not look upon him. Go with us.
Exeunt [Cleopatra, Enobarbus and the rest].
Mess. Fulvia thy wife first came into the field.
Ant. Against my brother Lucius?
Mess. Ay.
But soon that war had end, and the time's state
Made friends of them, jointing their force 'gainst Cæsar,
Whose better issue in the war from Italy
Upon the first encounter drave them.
Ant. Well, what worst?
Mess. The nature of bad news infects the teller.
Ant. When it concerns the fool or coward. On!
Things that are past are done with me. 'Tis thus:
Who tells me true, though in his tale lie death,
I hear him as he flattered.
Mess. Labienus—
This is stiff news—hath with his Parthian force
Extended Asia from Euphrates,

112. **Lydia:** a country in west central Asia Minor; **Ionia:** a portion of the western coast of Asia Minor, roughly from Smyrna to Miletus.

116-17. **home:** bluntly; **Mince not the general tongue:** mince no words in repeating what everyone says about me.

121-23. **then we bring forth weeds/When our quick minds lie still, and our ills told us/Is as our earing:** when we neglect to cultivate our reason, faults are our only products; but pointing out to us our faults is a remedy equivalent to earing (plowing) weed-grown soil. Plowing them under was one method of exterminating weeds.

126. **Sicyon:** a town in southern Greece where Antony knew Fulvia to be.

127. **stays upon:** awaits.

136. **Importeth thee to know:** concerns thee.

137. **Forbear me:** a polite request for the messenger's departure.

His conquering banner shook from Syria
To Lydia and to Ionia,
Whilst–

Ant. Antony, thou wouldst say.

Mess. O, my lord!

Ant. Speak to me home. Mince not the general tongue.
Name Cleopatra as she is called in Rome.
Rail thou in Fulvia's phrase, and taunt my faults
With such full license as both truth and malice
Have power to utter. O, then we bring forth weeds
When our quick minds lie still, and our ills told us
Is as our earing. Fare thee well awhile.

Mess. At your noble pleasure. *Exit.*

Ant. From Sicyon, ho, the news! Speak there!

1. Att. The man from Sicyon–is there such an one?

2. Att. He stays upon your will.

Ant. Let him appear.
These strong Egyptian fetters I must break
Or lose myself in dotage.

Enter another Messenger, with a letter.

What are you?

Mess. Fulvia thy wife is dead.

Ant. Where died she?

Mess. In Sicyon.
Her length of sickness, with what else more serious
Importeth thee to know, this bears.
[*Gives the letter.*]

Ant. Forbear me.
[*Exit Messenger.*]

141. **By revolution low'ring:** reaching a lower point on the wheel of Fortune. The regulation of human destinies by Fortune's wheel was a popular conception. Here Antony refers to the decline of a personal attitude or taste.

143. **could:** would willingly.

154. **were:** would be.

157. **noise:** rumor.

158. **moment:** cause.

159. **mettle:** ardent spirit.

Cleopatra—Jacobus de Strada, *Epitome thesauri antiquitatum* (1557)

There's a great spirit gone! Thus did I desire it.
What our contempts doth often hurl from us,
We wish it ours again. The present pleasure,
By revolution low'ring, does become
The opposite of itself. She's good, being gone;
The hand could pluck her back that shoved her on.
I must from this enchanting queen break off.
Ten thousand harms more than the ills I know
My idleness doth hatch. How now, Enobarbus!

[*Re-*]*enter Enobarbus.*

Eno. What's your pleasure, sir?

Ant. I must with haste from hence.

Eno. Why, then we kill all our women. We see how mortal an unkindness is to them. If they suffer our departure, death's the word.

Ant. I must be gone.

Eno. Under a compelling occasion let women die. It were pity to cast them away for nothing, though between them and a great cause they should be esteemed nothing. Cleopatra, catching but the least noise of this, dies instantly. I have seen her die twenty times upon far poorer moment. I do think there is mettle in death, which commits some loving act upon her, she hath such a celerity in dying.

Ant. She is cunning past man's thought.

Eno. Alack, sir, no! Her passions are made of nothing but the finest part of pure love. We cannot call her winds and waters sighs and tears. They are greater storms and tempests than almanacs can re-

171. **would have discredited your travel:** that is, if he had missed one of the world's wonders, his reputation as a traveler would have been marred.

187. **broached:** opened.

191. **abode:** remaining.

194. **expedience:** haste.

195. **leave:** Alexander Pope's emendation of the Folio "love"; **part:** depart.

196. **touches:** concerns.

port. This cannot be cunning in her; if it be, she makes a shower of rain as well as Jove.

Ant. Would I had never seen her!

Eno. O, sir, you had then left unseen a wonderful piece of work, which not to have been blest withal would have discredited your travel.

Ant. Fulvia is dead.

Eno. Sir?

Ant. Fulvia is dead.

Eno. Fulvia?

Ant. Dead.

Eno. Why, sir, give the gods a thankful sacrifice. When it pleaseth their deities to take the wife of a man from him, it shows to man the tailors of the earth; comforting therein, that when old robes are worn out, there are members to make new. If there were no more women but Fulvia, then had you indeed a cut, and the case to be lamented. This grief is crowned with consolation; your old smock brings forth a new petticoat; and indeed the tears live in an onion that should water this sorrow.

Ant. The business she hath broached in the state
Cannot endure my absence.

Eno. And the business you have broached here cannot be without you; especially that of Cleopatra's, which wholly depends on your abode.

Ant. No more light answers. Let our officers
Have notice what we purpose. I shall break
The cause of our expedience to the Queen
And get her leave to part. For not alone
The death of Fulvia, with more urgent touches,

199. **Petition us at home:** petition me to return home; **Sextus Pompeius:** youngest son of Gnæus Pompeius, known as Pompey the Great, who with Julius Cæsar and Marcus Crassus formed the first triumvirate in 60 B.C.

203-5. **throw/Pompey the Great and all his dignities/Upon his son:** i.e., credit Sextus Pompeius with a reputation as great as that earned by his father.

206-7. **blood and life:** high spirit and physical energy; **stands up/For the main soldier:** is acknowledged the very model of military excellence.

207-8. **whose quality, going on,/The sides o' the world may danger:** i.e., who will endanger the stability of the empire if he continues in his present course. **Quality** may mean either "personal characteristic" (his martial temperament) or "profession" (his military activity), both coming to much the same thing.

209-10. **like the courser's hair, hath yet but life/And not a serpent's poison:** a reference to the popular belief, still not altogether discredited, that a horsehair placed in water will change to a worm or snake.

210-12. **Say our pleasure/To such whose places under us require,/Our quick remove from hence:** tell the necessary subordinates of our wish for a speedy departure.

I. [iii.] 5. sad: grave, serious.

Do strongly speak to us, but the letters too
Of many our contriving friends in Rome
Petition us at home. Sextus Pompeius
Hath given the dare to Cæsar and commands
The empire of the sea. Our slippery people,
Whose love is never linked to the deserver
Till his deserts are past, begin to throw
Pompey the Great and all his dignities
Upon his son; who, high in name and power,
Higher than both in blood and life, stands up
For the main soldier; whose quality, going on,
The sides o' the world may danger. Much is breeding
Which, like the courser's hair, hath yet but life
And not a serpent's poison. Say our pleasure
To such whose places under us require,
Our quick remove from hence.

Eno. I shall do't. [*Exeunt.*]

[Scene III. Alexandria. Another room in Cleopatra's Palace.]

Enter Cleopatra, Charmian, Alexas, and Iras.

Cleo. Where is he?
Char. I did not see him since.
Cleo. See where he is, who's with him, what he does.
I did not send you. If you find him sad,
Say I am dancing; if in mirth, report
That I am sudden sick. Quick, and return!
[*Exit Alexas.*]

16. **I wish, forbear:** I would have you refrain altogether from being so provocative.

19. **sullen:** melancholy.

20. **breathing:** voice.

22. **the sides of nature:** i.e., her own natural strength.

Pompey the Great—Guillaume Rouillé, *Promptuarii iconum* (1553) (See I. ii. 204.)

Char. Madam, methinks if you did love him dearly,
You do not hold the method to enforce
The like from him.
Cleo. What should I do, I do not?
Char. In each thing give him way, cross him in nothing.
Cleo. Thou teachest like a fool. The way to lose him!
Char. Tempt him not so too far; I wish, forbear.
In time we hate that which we often fear.

Enter Antony.

But here comes Antony.
Cleo. I am sick and sullen.
Ant. I am sorry to give breathing to my purpose—
Cleo. Help me away, dear Charmian! I shall fall.
It cannot be thus long; the sides of nature
Will not sustain it.
Ant. Now, my dearest queen—
Cleo. Pray you stand farther from me.
Ant. What's the matter?
Cleo. I know by that same eye there's some good news.
What says the married woman? You may go.
Would she had never given you leave to come!
Let her not say 'tis I that keep you here.
I have no power upon you; hers you are.
Ant. The gods best know—
Cleo. O, never was there queen

41. **Riotous madness:** that is, it was raving madness for her.

42. **mouth-made vows:** vows that were mere words, since they did not come from the heart.

45. **color:** pretext.

46. **sued staying:** begged to be allowed to stay with me.

48. **our:** my, the royal plural.

49. **brows' bent:** eyebrows' arch; **parts:** physical characteristics.

50. **a race of heaven:** heavenly in origin, divine.

55. **a heart:** courage; **Egypt:** the Queen of Egypt.

59. **in use with you:** entrusted to you for your personal benefit, the legal sense of the word **use.**

60. **civil:** domestic.

61. **port:** harbor (Ostia).

62-3. **Equality of two domestic powers/Breed scrupulous faction:** the two domestic parties are so evenly matched that the uncommitted are cautious about joining either side. **Scrupulous** means "cautious" here.

So mightily betrayed! Yet at the first
I saw the treasons planted.
Ant. Cleopatra—
Cleo. Why should I think you can be mine, and true,
Though you in swearing shake the throned gods,
Who have been false to Fulvia? Riotous madness,
To be entangled with those mouth-made vows
Which break themselves in swearing!
Ant. Most sweet queen—
Cleo. Nay, pray you seek no color for your going,
But bid farewell and go. When you sued staying,
Then was the time for words. No going then!
Eternity was in our lips and eyes,
Bliss in our brows' bent, none our parts so poor
But was a race of heaven. They are so still,
Or thou, the greatest soldier of the world,
Art turned the greatest liar.
Ant. How now, lady?
Cleo. I would I had thy inches! Thou shouldst know
There were a heart in Egypt.
Ant. Hear me, Queen.
The strong necessity of time commands
Our services awhile; but my full heart
Remains in use with you. Our Italy
Shines o'er with civil swords. Sextus Pompeius
Makes his approaches to the port of Rome.
Equality of two domestic powers
Breed scrupulous faction. The hated, grown to strength,
Are newly grown to love. The condemned Pompey,

66. **apace:** speedily.

68. **Upon the present state:** under the present rule of the triumvirs; **whose:** referring to "such as have not thrived."

69. **purge:** cure itself.

70. **particular:** personal motive.

71. **safe my going:** make my going appear safe to you.

77. **at thy sovereign leisure:** at such time as pleases you (who have absolute freedom to choose how you spend your time).

78. **garboils:** disorders, upheavals.

86. **the fire:** i.e., the sun.

87. **quickens:** revives and renews the fertility of.

89. **affects:** prefer.

91-2. **I am quickly ill and well—/So Antony loves:** my health depends on whether Antony loves me. In short, Cleopatra will be perfectly all right if Antony will only express his love with sufficient conviction.

94. **give true evidence:** testify truly; i.e., admit that he loves you.

Rich in his father's honor, creeps apace
Into the hearts of such as have not thrived
Upon the present state, whose numbers threaten;
And quietness, grown sick of rest, would purge
By any desperate change. My more particular,
And that which most with you should safe my going,
Is Fulvia's death.
Cleo. Though age from folly could not give me freedom,
It does from childishness. Can Fulvia die?
Ant. She's dead, my queen.
Look here, and at thy sovereign leisure read
The garboils she awaked. At the last, best,
See when and where she died.
Cleo. O most false love!
Where be the sacred vials thou shouldst fill
With sorrowful watcr? Now I see, I see,
In Fulvia's death, how mine received shall be.
Ant. Quarrel no more, but be prepared to know
The purposes I bear; which are, or cease,
As you shall give the advice. By thc fire
That quickens Nilus' slime, I go from hence
Thy soldier, servant, making peace or war
As thou affects.
Cleo. Cut my laoe, Charmian, come!
But let it be. I am quickly ill and well—
So Antony loves.
Ant. My precious queen, forbear,
And give true evidence to his love, which stands
An honorable trial.

99. **Good now:** if you'll be so good; see I. [ii.] 27.

101. **honor:** honesty.

103. **meetly:** moderately well acted.

105. **target:** shield; **Still he mends:** he continues to improve.

107-8. **Herculean:** Antony claimed descent from the hero Hercules; **does become/The carriage of his chafe:** i.e., carries off his pretense of anger.

114. **my oblivion is a very Antony:** I am forgetful in the same degree as Antony is faithless.

116-18. **But that your royalty/Holds idleness your subject, I should take you/For idleness itself:** if you were not so well able to command folly to serve you, I should think you the personification of folly. In other words, caprice is one of Cleopatra's charms, and she knows it well.

119-20. **'Tis sweating labor/To bear such idleness so near the heart:** it is painful to play the fool about a matter so dear to me. Cleopatra identifies **idleness** with Antony and thus makes a *double-entendre.*

122-23. **my becomings kill me when they do not/Eye well to you:** even my most admirable qualities are my enemies when they displease you.

Hercules—Guillaume Rouillé, *Promptuarii iconum* (1553)

Cleo. So Fulvia told me.
I prithee turn aside and weep for her;
Then bid adieu to me, and say the tears
Belong to Egypt. Good now, play one scene
Of excellent dissembling, and let it look
Like perfect honor.
Ant. You'll heat my blood. No more!
Cleo. You can do better yet; but this is meetly.
Ant. Now by my sword—
Cleo. And target. Still he mends;
But this is not the best. Look, prithee, Charmian,
How this Herculean Roman does become
The carriage of his chafe.
Ant. I'll leave you, lady.
Cleo. Courteous lord, one word.
Sir, you and I must part—but that's not it.
Sir, you and I have loved—but there's not it.
That you know well. Something it is I would—
O, my oblivion is a very Antony,
And I am all forgotten!
Ant. But that your royalty
Holds idleness your subject, I should take you
For idleness itself.
Cleo. 'Tis sweating labor
To bear such idleness so near the heart
As Cleopatra this. But, sir, forgive me;
Since my becomings kill me when they do not
Eye well to you. Your honor calls you hence;
Therefore be deaf to my unpitied folly,
And all the gods go with you! Upon your sword

I. [iv.] 3. Our: an editorial correction of the Folio reading "One"; **competitor:** associate.

6. **Ptolemy:** Cleopatra's brother, now dead, to whom she had been married in accordance with Egyptian custom.

7. **gave audience:** i.e., to Cæsar's messengers.

8. **Vouchsafed:** condescended.

10. **abstract:** epitome.

13. **enow:** enough.

14. **His faults . . . seem as the spots of heaven:** that is, as the stars are set off by the blackness of the sky, Antony's faults stand out in striking contrast to his virtues.

Octavius Cæsar as the Emperor Augustus—Giovanni Battista Cavallerüs, *Romanorum imperatorum effigies* (1590)

Sit laurel victory, and smooth success
Be strewed before your feet!

Ant. Let us go. Come.
Our separation so abides and flies
That thou, residing here, goes yet with me,
And I, hence fleeting, here remain with thee.
Away!

Exeunt.

[Scene IV. Rome. Cæsar's house.]

Enter Octavius [*Cæsar*], *reading a letter, Lepidus, and their Train.*

Cæs. You may see, Lepidus, and henceforth know,
It is not Cæsar's natural vice to hate
Our great competitor. From Alexandria
This is the news: he fishes, drinks, and wastes
The lamps of night in revel; is not more manlike
Than Cleopatra, nor the queen of Ptolemy
More womanly than he; hardly gave audience, or
Vouchsafed to think he had partners. You shall find there
A man who is the abstract of all faults
That all men follow.

Lep. I must not think there are
Evils enow to darken all his goodness.
His faults, in him, seem as the spots of heaven,
More fiery by night's blackness; hereditary

16. **purchased:** acquired.

20. **for a mirth:** in exchange for diversion.

21. **keep the turn of tippling:** match drink for drink.

22-3. **stand the buffet/With knaves:** mingle with common men.

24-5. **As his composure must be rare indeed/Whom these things cannot blemish:** although only an extraordinary man could fail to be marred by such deeds.

26-7. **foils:** disgraces, shortcomings; **we do bear/So great weight in his lightness:** his trifling affects us so greatly.

28. **vacancy:** i.e., only his spare time.

29-30. **surfeits and the dryness of his bones/Call on him for't:** the consequent physical ailments might be his only punishment; **confound:** waste; see I. i. 53.

31-2. **drums him from his sport:** i.e., should call him from pleasure like the urgent summons of a martial drum; **speaks as loud/As his own state and ours:** is as important as his own personal position and the safety of the whole government.

33. **rate:** scold.

34-5. **Pawn their experience to their present pleasure/And so rebel to judgment:** risk losing the benefits of their experience by yielding to pleasure, and in this way oppose their own better judgment.

43. **discontents:** malcontents; **repair:** go.

44. **Give:** assert.

Rather than purchased; what he cannot change
Than what he chooses.

Cæs. You are too indulgent. Let's grant it is not
Amiss to tumble on the bed of Ptolemy,
To give a kingdom for a mirth, to sit
And keep the turn of tippling with a slave,
To reel the streets at noon, and stand the buffet
With knaves that smell of sweat. Say this becomes him
(As his composure must be rare indeed
Whom these things cannot blemish), yet must Antony
No way excuse his foils when we do bear
So great weight in his lightness. If he filled
His vacancy with his voluptuousness,
Full surfeits and the dryness of his bones
Call on him for't! But to confound such time
That drums him from his sport and speaks as loud
As his own state and ours—'tis to be chid
As we rate boys who, being mature in knowledge,
Pawn their experience to their present pleasure
And so rebel to judgment.

Enter a Messenger.

Lep. Here's more news.

Mess. Thy biddings have been done, and every hour,
Most noble Cæsar, shalt thou have report
How 'tis abroad. Pompey is strong at sea,
And it appears he is beloved of those
That only have feared Cæsar. To the ports
The discontents repair, and men's reports
Give him much wronged.

46. **primal state:** first government.

47-9. **he which is was wished until he were;/ And the ebbed man, ne'er loved till ne'er worth love,/ Comes deared by being lacked: he which is** (the man of power) is desired until he attains power, while **the ebbed man** (one declined in power), who is never loved until it is no longer worthwhile to love him, becomes beloved upon his downfall. In other words, power and popularity do not go together. **Deared** is Theobald's correction of the Folio reading "fear'd."

50. **vagabond flag:** wild iris.

51. **lackeying:** following, as a servant (lackey) does his master. This is Theobald's reading for the Folio "lacking."

55. **ear:** plow, as at I. [ii.] 123.

58. **blood:** courage; **flush youth revolt:** i.e., the youthful and spirited join the pirates instead of defending the country against them.

60-1. **Pompey's name strikes more/Than could his war resisted:** Pompey's name has more force than his military strength could possess (even if it were) resisted.

63. **wassails:** carousings.

64. **Modena:** a city and province in north central Italy.

69. **stale:** urine; **gilded:** covered with scum.

Cæs. I should have known no less.
It hath been taught us from the primal state
That he which is was wished until he were;
And the ebbed man, ne'er loved till ne'er worth love,
Comes deared by being lacked. This common body,
Like to a vagabond flag upon the stream,
Goes to and back, lackeying the varying tide,
To rot itself with motion.
Mess. Cæsar, I bring thee word,
Menecrates and Menas, famous pirates,
Makes the sea serve them, which they ear and wound
With keels of every kind. Many hot inroads
They make in Italy; the borders maritime
Lack blood to think on't, and flush youth revolt.
No vessel can peep forth but 'tis as soon
Taken as seen; for Pompey's name strikes more
Than could his war resisted.
Cæs. Antony,
Leave thy lascivious wassails. When thou once
Wast beaten from Modena, where thou slewst
Hirtius and Pansa, consuls, at thy heel
Did famine follow, whom thou foughtst against
(Though daintily brought up) with patience more
Than savages could suffer. Thou didst drink
The stale of horses and the gilded puddle
Which beasts would cough at. Thy palate then did deign
The roughest berry on the rudest hedge.
Yea, like the stag when snow the pasture sheets,
The barks of trees thou browsedst. On the Alps
It is reported thou didst eat strange flesh,

79. **lanked:** thinned.

80. **pity of him:** a pity about him.

87. **furnished:** supplied with the necessary information.

88-9. **what by sea and land I can be able/To front this present time:** what naval and military powers I will have to oppose the present crisis.

97. **bond:** duty.

Roman soldiers—Guillaume Du Choul, *Discours de la religion des anciens Romains* (1556)

Which some did die to look on. And all this
(It wounds thine honor that I speak it now)
Was borne so like a soldier that thy cheek
So much as lanked not.

Lep. 'Tis pity of him.

Cæs. Let his shames quickly
Drive him to Rome. 'Tis time we twain
Did show ourselves i' the field, and to that end
Assemble we immediate council. Pompey
Thrives in our idleness.

Lep. Tomorrow, Cæsar,
I shall be furnished to inform you rightly
Both what by sea and land I can be able
To front this present time.

Cæs. Till which encounter,
It is my business too. Farewell.

Lep. Farewell, my lord. What you shall know meantime
Of stirs abroad, I shall beseech you, sir,
To let me be partaker.

Cæs. Doubt not, sir;
I knew it for my bond.

Exeunt.

I. [v.] 4. mandragora: a plant whose root was used for sleeping potions.

15. **unseminared:** castrated.

16. **May not fly forth of Egypt:** i.e., are not drawn, as mine are, to an absent lover; **affections:** passionate inclinations.

20. **honest:** chaste, with a pun on the usual meaning.

[Scene V. Alexandria. A room in Cleopatra's Palace.]

Enter Cleopatra, Charmian, Iras, and Mardian.

Cleo. Charmian!
Char. Madam?
Cleo. Ha, ha!
Give me to drink mandragora.
Char. Why, madam?
Cleo. That I might sleep out this great gap of time
My Antony is away.
Char. You think of him too much.
Cleo. O, 'tis treason!
Char. Madam, I trust not so.
Cleo. Thou, eunuch Mardian!
Mar. What's your Highness' pleasure?
Cleo. Not now to hear thee sing. I take no pleasure
In aught an eunuch has. 'Tis well for thee
That, being unseminared, thy freer thoughts
May not fly forth of Egypt. Hast thou affections?
Mar. Yes, gracious madam.
Cleo. Indeed?
Mar. Not in deed, madam; for I can do nothing
But what indeed is honest to be done.
Yet have I fierce affections, and think
What Venus did with Mars.
Cleo. O, Charmian!
Where thinkst thou he is now? Stands he, or sits he?
Or does he walk? or is he on his horse?
O happy horse, to bear the weight of Antony!

27. **wotst:** knowest.

28-9. **demi-Atlas:** i.e., the hero who supports half the world on his shoulders. Presumably Cleopatra gives Cæsar credit for supporting the other half—Lepidus is discounted by everyone; **the arm/And burgonet of men:** mankind's model warrior. A **burgonet** is a helmet.

33. **am with Phoebus' amorous pinches black:** am darkened by the sun's touches. Cleopatra's description of herself is, of course, not to be taken too literally.

34. **Broad-fronted:** having a broad forehead, an allusion to his great capacity.

36. **great Pompey:** historically, Gnæus Pompeius the younger, not Pompey the Great. Shakespeare does not make the distinction and probably confused the two.

38. **aspect:** gaze.

42. **that great med'cine:** i.e., his great power has transmuted you, in the same way as the alchemist's tincture was supposed to transmute baser metals into gold.

44. **brave:** splendid.

47. **orient:** lustrous.

50. **firm:** faithful; **great Egypt:** the Queen of Egypt, as before.

52. **piece:** add to.

Do bravely, horse! for wotst thou whom thou movest?
The demi-Atlas of this earth, the arm
And burgonet of men. He's speaking now,
Or murmuring "Where's my serpent of old Nile?"
For so he calls me. Now I feed myself
With most delicious poison. Think on me,
That am with Phoebus' amorous pinches black
And wrinkled deep in time. Broad-fronted Cæsar,
When thou wast here above the ground, I was
A morsel for a monarch; and great Pompey
Would stand and make his eyes grow in my brow;
There would he anchor his aspect, and die
With looking on his life.

Enter Alexas.

Alex. Sovereign of Egypt, hail!
Cleo. How much unlike art thou Mark Antony!
Yet, coming from him, that great med'cine hath
With his tinct gilded thee.
How goes it with my brave Mark Antony?
Alex. Last thing he did, dear Queen,
He kissed—the last of many doubled kisses—
This orient pearl. His speech sticks in my heart.
Cleo. Mine ear must pluck it thence.
Alex. "Good friend," quoth he,
"Say the firm Roman to great Egypt sends
This treasure of an oyster; at whose foot,
To mend the petty present, I will piece
Her opulent throne with kingdoms. All the East,
Say thou, shall call her mistress." So he nodded,

55. **arm-gaunt:** the precise meaning is uncertain. **Gaunt** can mean "trained to leanness" and **arm** "armored." The intent is to portray a business-like Antony mounting a war horse.

57. **dumbed:** silenced; i.e., his words were drowned out.

61. **nor . . . nor:** neither . . . nor.

63. **'tis the man; but note him:** "that's Antony all right; just observe how he conducts himself."

70. **posts:** messengers riding posthaste.

71. **several:** separate.

75. **Shall die a beggar:** i.e., it will be an ill day indeed.

83. **paragon:** compare, parallel.

Julius Cæsar—Giovanni Battista Cavallerüs, *Romanorum imperatorum effigies* (1590)

And soberly did mount an arm-gaunt steed,
Who neighed so high that what I would have spoke
Was beastly dumbed by him.
Cleo. What, was he sad or merry?
Alex. Like to the time o' the year between the extremes
Of hot and cold. He was nor sad nor merry.
Cleo. O well-divided disposition! Note him,
Note him, good Charmian; 'tis the man; but note him!
He was not sad, for he would shine on those
That make their looks by his; he was not merry,
Which seemed to tell them his remembrance lay
In Egypt with his joy; but between both.
O heavenly mingle! Beest thou sad or merry,
The violence of either thee becomes,
So does it no man else.—Metst thou my posts?
Alex. Ay, madam, twenty several messengers.
Why do you send so thick?
Cleo. Who's born that day
When I forget to send to Antony
Shall die a beggar. Ink and paper, Charmian.
Welcome, my good Alexas. Did I, Charmian,
Ever love Cæsar so?
Char. O that brave Cæsar!
Cleo. Be choked with such another emphasis!
Say "the brave Antony."
Char. The valiant Cæsar!
Cleo. By Isis, I will give thee bloody teeth
If thou with Cæsar paragon again
My man of men!

86. **I sing but after you:** that is, I am only echoing what you yourself once said.

Roman horseman–Guillaume Du Choul, *Discours de la religion des anciens Romains* (1556) (See I. v. 55.)

Char. By your most gracious pardon,
I sing but after you.
Cleo. My salad days,
When I was green in judgment, cold in blood,
To say as I said then. But come, away!
Get me ink and paper.
He shall have every day a several greeting,
Or I'll unpeople Egypt.

Exeunt.

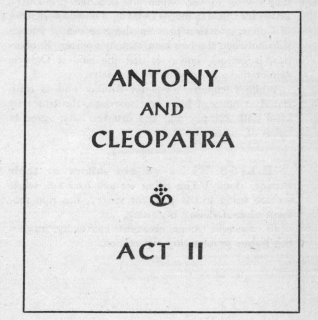

ANTONY AND CLEOPATRA

ACT II

[II.] Though Pompey and his allies (the pirates Menas and Menecrates) are hopeful that Antony's defection and probable rupture with his fellow triumvirs will ensure their own success, Antony makes his peace with Cæsar and Lepidus. The death of Antony's wife, Fulvia, which had occurred previously, leaves him free to marry Octavia, the widowed sister of Cæsar, and thus to strengthen the ties of friendship between the two men. Antony's officer, Enobarbus, is certain, however, that the modest Octavia cannot make Antony forget Cleopatra.

While Cleopatra longs for Antony and is infuriated at news of his recent marriage, the triumvirs meet with Pompey and at a drunken feast agree to terms of peace.

[II. i.] 5-6. **Whiles we are suitors to their throne, decays/The thing we sue for:** i.e., while we are suing to the gods for victory, the ripe moment to gain victory is passing.

13. **powers:** troops; **crescent:** increasing; **auguring hope:** prophesying expectation.

[ACT II]

[Scene I. Messina. Pompey's house.]

Enter Pompey, Menecrates, and Menas, in warlike manner.

Pom. If the great gods be just, they shall assist
The deeds of justest men.
Menec. Know, worthy Pompey,
That what they do delay, they not deny.
Pom. Whiles we are suitors to their throne, decays
The thing we sue for.
Menec. We, ignorant of ourselves,
Beg often our own harms, which the wise pow'rs
Deny us for our good: so find we profit
By losing of our prayers.
Pom. I shall do well.
The people love me, and the sea is mine;
My powers are crescent, and my auguring hope
Says it will come to the full. Mark Antony
In Egypt sits at dinner, and will make
No wars without doors. Cæsar gets money where
He loses hearts. Lepidus flatters both,
Of both is flattered; but he neither loves,
Nor either cares for him.

27. **Salt:** lustful; **waned:** that is, waned from its earlier perfection.

31. **cloyless:** noncloying.

32-3. **prorogue his honor/Even till a Lethe'd dullness:** delay his remembrance of honor, just as though he had drunk of the river Lethe (which caused complete oblivion in the drinker).

37-8. **Since he went from Egypt 'tis/A space for farther travel:** enough time has elapsed since he left Egypt to have traveled a greater distance.

44. **opinion:** self-esteem.

45. **Egypt's widow:** i.e., the widow of Egypt's King; see note at I. [iv.] 6.

Menas. Cæsar and Lepidus
Are in the field; a mighty strength they carry.
Pom. Where have you this? 'Tis false.
Menas. From Silvius, sir.
Pom. He dreams. I know they are in Rome together,
Looking for Antony. But all the charms of love,
Salt Cleopatra, soften thy waned lip!
Let witchcraft join with beauty, lust with both!
Tie up the libertine in a field of feasts,
Keep his brain fuming. Epicurean cooks
Sharpen with cloyless sauce his appetite,
That sleep and feeding may prorogue his honor
Even till a Lethe'd dullness!

Enter Varrius.

How now, Varrius?
Var. This is most certain that I shall deliver:
Mark Antony is every hour in Rome
Expected. Since he went from Egypt 'tis
A space for farther travel.
Pom. I could have given less matter
A better ear. Menas, I did not think
This amorous surfeiter would have donned his helm
For such a petty war. His soldiership
Is twice the other twain. But let us rear
The higher our opinion, that our stirring
Can from the lap of Egypt's widow pluck
The ne'er-lust-wearied Antony.

47. **hope:** expect.

48. **well greet together:** meet with mutual cordiality.

55. **'Twere:** it would be; **pregnant:** big with consequence, extremely probable; **square:** fall out, quarrel.

61-2. **stands/Our lives upon:** is of vital concern to us.

Menas. I cannot hope
Cæsar and Antony shall well greet together.
His wife that's dead did trespasses to Cæsar;
His brother warred upon him; although, I think,
Not moved by Antony.
Pom. I know not, Menas,
How lesser enmities may give way to greater.
Were't not that we stand up against them all,
'Twere pregnant they should square between themselves,
For they have entertained cause enough
To draw their swords; but how the fear of us
May cement their divisions and bind up
The petty difference we yet not know.
Be't as our gods will have't! It only stands
Our lives upon to use our strongest hands.
Come, Menas.

Exeunt.

[Scene II. Rome. The house of Lepidus.]

Enter Enobarbus and Lepidus.

Lep. Good Enobarbus, 'tis a worthy deed,
And shall become you well, to entreat your captain
To soft and gentle speech.
Eno. I shall entreat him
To answer like himself. If Cæsar move him,
Let Antony look over Cæsar's head
And speak as loud as Mars. By Jupiter,

[II. ii.] 11. **stomaching:** enmity.

20. **compose:** reach agreement.

26. **leaner:** slighter.

28-9. **commit/Murder in healing wounds:** make slight wounds deadly.

30. **The rather for:** all the more because.

32. **Nor curstness grow to the matter:** nor let ill temper accompany the discussion.

The triumvirs, Cæsar, Antony, and Lepidus—Jacobus de Strada, ***Epitome thesauri antiquitatum*** **(1557)**

Were I the wearer of Antonius' beard,
I would not shave't today!
Lep. 'Tis not a time
For private stomaching.
Eno. Every time
Serves for the matter that is then born in't.
Lep. But small to greater matters must give way.
Eno. Not if the small come first.
Lep. Your speech is passion;
But pray you stir no embers up. Here comes
The noble Antony.

Enter Antony and Ventidius.

Eno. And yonder, Cæsar.

Enter Cæsar, Mæcenas, and Agrippa.

Ant. If we compose well here, to Parthia.
Hark, Ventidius.
Cæs. I do not know,
Mæcenas. Ask Agrippa.
Lep. Noble friends,
That which combined us was most great, and let not
A leaner action rend us. What's amiss,
May it be gently heard. When we debate
Our trivial difference loud, we do commit
Murder in healing wounds. Then, noble partners,
The rather for I earnestly beseech,
Touch you the sourest points with sweetest terms,
Nor curstness grow to the matter.

S.D. at l. 35. **Flourish:** probably a gesture of salute with his sword.

41-2. **take things ill which are not so,/Or being, concern you not:** take offense at false reports, which would be none of your business even if they were true.

43. **must:** should.

44. **or . . . or:** either . . . or.

47. **derogately:** in a derogatory manner, disparagingly.

53. **practice on:** plot against.

54. **question:** concern.

59. **Was theme for you; you were the word of war:** i.e., you were the reason; the war was made in your name.

Ant. 'Tis spoken well.
Were we before our armies, and to fight,
I should do thus. *Flourish.*
Cæs. Welcome to Rome.
Ant. Thank you.
Cæs. Sit.
Ant. Sit, sir.
Cæs. Nay then.

[*They seat themselves.*]

Ant. I learn you take things ill which are not so,
Or being, concern you not.
Cæs. I must be laughed at
If, or for nothing or a little, I
Should say myself offended, and with you
Chiefly i' the world; more laughed at that I should
Once name you derogately when to sound your name
It not concerned me.
Ant. My being in Egypt, Cæsar,
What was't to you?
Cæs. No more than my residing here at Rome
Might be to you in Egypt. Yet if you there
Did practice on my state, your being in Egypt
Might be my question.
Ant. How intend you, practiced?
Cæs. You may be pleased to catch at mine intent
By what did here befall me. Your wife and brother
Made wars upon me, and their contestation
Was theme for you; you were the word of war.

60. **do mistake your business:** are mistaken about this matter.

62. **urge:** mention.

63. **true reports:** honest informants.

66. **stomach:** desire, inclination.

68. **satisfy:** fully inform; **patch:** improvise from scraps.

69. **As:** whereas.

78. **with graceful eyes attend:** regard favorably, approve.

79. **fronted:** opposed, as at I. [iv.] 89.

81-2. **with a snaffle/You may pace easy:** you may control by means of a bridle—a technical metaphor from horsemanship.

Ant. You do mistake your business. My brother never
Did urge me in his act. I did inquire it
And have my learning from some true reports
That drew their swords with you. Did he not rather
Discredit my authority with yours,
And make the wars alike against my stomach,
Having alike your cause? Of this my letters
Before did satisfy you. If you'll patch a quarrel,
As matter whole you have to make it with,
It must not be with this.

Cæs. You praise yourself
By laying defects of judgment to me; but
You patched up your excuses.

Ant. Not so, not so!
I know you could not lack, I am certain on't,
Very necessity of this thought, that I,
Your partner in the cause 'gainst which he fought,
Could not with graceful eyes attend those wars
Which fronted mine own peace. As for my wife,
I would you had her spirit in such another!
The third o' the world is yours, which with a snaffle
You may pace easy, but not such a wife.

Eno. Would we had all such wives, that the men might go to wars with the women!

Ant. So much uncurbable, her garboils, Cæsar,
Made out of her impatience—which not wanted
Shrewdness of policy too—I grieving grant
Did you too much disquiet. For that you must
But say I could not help it.

93. **missive:** messenger.

96-7. **did want/Of what I was i' the morning:** i.e., was not quite myself.

98. **told him of myself:** explained my condition.

108. **on:** of.

117-19. **mine honesty/Shall not make poor my greatness, nor my power/Work without it:** my honor (which compels me to confess my fault) will not allow me to be abject in my apologies, nor can I retain my power without honor.

Cæs. I wrote to you
When, rioting in Alexandria, you
Did pocket up my letters, and with taunts
Did gibe my missive out of audience.
Ant. Sir,
He fell upon me ere admitted. Then
Three kings I had newly feasted, and did want
Of what I was i' the morning; but next day
I told him of myself, which was as much
As to have asked him pardon. Let this fellow
Be nothing of our strife. If we contend,
Out of our question wipe him.
Cæs. You have broken
The article of your oath, which you shall never
Have tongue to charge me with.
Lep. Soft, Cæsar!
Ant. No,
Lepidus; let him speak.
The honor is sacred which he talks on now,
Supposing that I lacked it. But on, Cæsar.
The article of my oath–
Cæs. To lend me arms and aid when I required them,
The which you both denied.
Ant. Neglected rather;
And then when poisoned hours had bound me up
From mine own knowledge. As nearly as I may,
I'll play the penitent to you; but mine honesty
Shall not make poor my greatness, nor my power
Work without it. Truth is, that Fulvia,
To have me out of Egypt, made wars here,

125. **enforce:** urge.

128. **atone:** reconcile.

134. **a soldier only:** that is, "and know nothing of diplomacy."

139. **Go to, then! your considerate stone:** "Very well! I will be as dumb as a stone to please you (but at the same time I will continue to weigh the circumstances and come to my own conclusions about them)." Enobarbus uses the word **considerate** with deliberate ambiguity.

142-43. **our conditions/So diff'ring in their acts:** in view of the fact that our temperaments are so unlike.

For which myself, the ignorant motive, do
So far ask pardon as befits mine honor
To stoop in such a case.

Lep. 'Tis noble spoken.

Mæc. If it might please you to enforce no further
The griefs between ye—to forget them quite
Were to remember that the present need
Speaks to atone you.

Lep. Worthily spoken, Mæcenas.

Eno. Or, if you borrow one another's love for the instant, you may, when you hear no more words of Pompey, return it again. You shall have time to wrangle in when you have nothing else to do.

Ant. Thou art a soldier only. Speak no more.

Eno. That truth should be silent I had almost forgot.

Ant. You wrong this presence; therefore speak no more.

Eno. Go to, then! your considerate stone.

Cæs. I do not much dislike the matter, but
The manner of his speech; for 't cannot be
We shall remain in friendship, our conditions
So diff'ring in their acts. Yet if I knew
What hoop should hold us staunch, from edge to edge
O' the world I would pursue it.

Agr. Give me leave, Cæsar.

Cæs. Speak, Agrippa.

Agr. Thou hast a sister by the mother's side,
Admired Octavia. Great Mark Antony
Is now a widower.

153. **reproof:** Thomas Hanmer's reading for the Folio "proof."

162-63. **speak/That which none else can utter:** speak more eloquently for themselves than others could praise them.

164. **jealousies:** suspicions.

165. **import their dangers:** carry their own dangers with them; i.e., are all dangerous.

173. **touched:** affected.

181. **so fairly shows:** appears so fair.

Cæs. Say not so, Agrippa.
If Cleopatra heard you, your reproof
Were well deserved of rashness.
Ant. I am not married, Cæsar. Let me hear
Agrippa further speak.
Agr. To hold you in perpetual amity,
To make you brothers, and to knit your hearts
With an unslipping knot, take Antony
Octavia to his wife; whose beauty claims
No worse a husband than the best of men;
Whose virtue and whose general graces speak
That which none else can utter. By this marriage
All little jealousies, which now seem great,
And all great fears, which now import their dangers,
Would then be nothing. Truths would be tales,
Where now half-tales be truths. Her love to both
Would each to other, and all loves to both,
Draw after her. Pardon what I have spoke;
For 'tis a studied, not a present thought,
By duty ruminated.
Ant. Will Cæsar speak?
Cæs. Not till he hears how Antony is touched
With what is spoke already.
Ant. What power is in Agrippa,
If I would say "Agrippa, be it so,"
To make this good?
Cæs. The power of Cæsar, and
His power unto Octavia.
Ant. May I never
To this good purpose, that so fairly shows,
Dream of impediment! Let me have thy hand.

189-90. **never/Fly off our loves again:** may our friendship never falter.

194. **strange:** extraordinary.

198. **upon's:** upon us.

199. **presently:** immediately.

202. **Mount Misenum:** a promontory at the west of the Bay of Naples.

206. **So is the fame:** so Rumor has it.

212. **straight:** directly, at once.

Further this act of grace; and from this hour
The heart of brothers govern in our loves
And sway our great designs!
Cæs. There is my hand.
A sister I bequeath you, whom no brother
Did ever love so dearly. Let her live
To join our kingdoms and our hearts; and never
Fly off our loves again!
Lep. Happily, amen!
Ant. I did not think to draw my sword 'gainst Pompey;
For he hath laid strange courtesies and great
Of late upon me. I must thank him only,
Lest my remembrance suffer ill report;
At heel of that, defy him.
Lep. Time calls upon's.
Of us must Pompey presently be sought,
Or else he seeks out us.
Ant. Where lies he?
Cæs. About the Mount Misenum.
Ant. What is his strength by land?
Cæs. Great and increasing; but by sea
He is an absolute master.
Ant. So is the fame.
Would we had spoke together! Haste we for it.
Yet, ere we put ourselves in arms, dispatch we
The business we have talked of.
Cæs. With most gladness;
And do invite you to my sister's view,
Whither straight I'll lead you.

S.D. after l. 216. **Flourish:** a series of notes on the trumpet.

218. **Half the heart of Cæsar:** a complimentary allusion to Mæcenas' place in Cæsar's favor.

222. **disgested:** settled.

230. **triumphant:** spectacular.

231. **square:** precise, correct.

232-33. **pursed up:** pocketed.

234. **appeared indeed:** a word has evidently dropped out here. Agrippa means that she made a glorious appearance.

Ant. Let us, Lepidus,
Not lack your company.

Lep. Noble Antony,
Not sickness should detain me.

Flourish. Exeunt. Manent Enobarbus, Agrippa, Mæcenas.

Mæc. Welcome from Egypt, sir.

Eno. Half the heart of Cæsar, worthy Mæcenas!
My honorable friend, Agrippa!

Agr. Good Enobarbus!

Mæc. We have cause to be glad that matters are so well disgested. You stayed well by't in Egypt.

Eno. Ay, sir; we did sleep day out of countenance and made the night light with drinking.

Mæc. Eight wild boars roasted whole at a breakfast, and but twelve persons there. Is this true?

Eno. This was but as a fly by an eagle. We had much more monstrous matter of feast, which worthily deserved noting.

Mæc. She's a most triumphant lady, if report be square to her.

Eno. When she first met Mark Antony, she pursed up his heart, upon the river of Cydnus.

Agr. There she appeared indeed; or my reporter devised well for her.

Eno. I will tell you.
The barge she sat in, like a burnished throne,
Burned on the water. The poop was beaten gold;
Purple the sails, and so perfumed that
The winds were lovesick with them; the oars were silver,

246. **cloth-of-gold of tissue:** a rich fabric of silk woven with gold threads.

247-48. **O'erpicturing that Venus where we see/The fancy outwork nature:** that is, presenting a picture of Venus more beautiful than any woman nature could produce. There has been some speculation as to what representation of Venus Shakespeare may have had in mind, but since Plutarch says that Cleopatra was "appareled and attired like the goddess Venus, commonly drawn in picture," it is probable that no specific picture was in Shakespeare's mind.

254. **Nereides:** sea nymphs, daughters of Nereus, a water god; pronounced as three syllables in this spelling.

255, 256. **eyes, bends:** nautical terms for parts of the rigging and bulwarks. Shakespeare describes the attendants as standing on either side of the barge dressed like mermaids, and thus adorning that portion of the barge.

259. **yarely:** skillfully; **frame:** perform; **office:** function; see I. i. 5.

Which to the tune of flutes kept stroke, and made
The water which they beat to follow faster,
As amorous of their strokes. For her own person,
It beggared all description. She did lie
In her pavilion, cloth-of-gold of tissue,
O'erpicturing that Venus where we see
The fancy outwork nature. On each side her
Stood pretty dimpled boys, like smiling Cupids,
With divers-colored fans, whose wind did seem
To glow the delicate cheeks which they did cool,
And what they undid did.

Agr. O, rare for Antony!

Eno. Her gentlewomen, like the Nereides,
So many mermaids, tended her i' the eyes,
And made their bends adornings. At the helm
A seeming mermaid steers. The silken tackle
Swell with the touches of those flower-soft hands
That yarely frame the office. From the barge
A strange invisible perfume hits the sense
Of the adjacent wharfs. The city cast
Her people out upon her; and Antony,
Enthroned i' the market place, did sit alone,
Whistling to the air; which, but for vacancy,
Had gone to gaze on Cleopatra too,
And made a gap in nature.

Agr. Rare Egyptian!

Eno. Upon her landing, Antony sent to her,
Invited her to supper. She replied,
It should be better he became her guest;
Which she entreated. Our courteous Antony,
Whom ne'er the word of "no" woman heard speak,

274. **ordinary:** meal. A set meal available at the public table of a tavern or inn was called an **ordinary.**

286. **custom:** familiarity.

291. **riggish:** wanton.

294. **lottery:** prize.

Being barbered ten times o'er, goes to the feast,
And for his ordinary pays his heart
For what his eyes eat only.

Agr. Royal wench!
She made great Cæsar lay his sword to bed.
He plowed her, and she cropped.

Eno. I saw her once
Hop forty paces through the public street;
And having lost her breath, she spoke, and panted,
That she did make defect perfection
And, breathless, pow'r breathe forth.

Mæc. Now Antony must leave her utterly.

Eno. Never! He will not.
Age cannot wither her nor custom stale
Her infinite variety. Other women cloy
The appetites they feed, but she makes hungry
Where most she satisfies; for vilest things
Become themselves in her, that the holy priests
Bless her when she is riggish.

Mæc. If beauty, wisdom, modesty, can settle
The heart of Antony, Octavia is
A blessed lottery to him.

Agr. Let us go.
Good Enobarbus, make yourself my guest
Whilst you abide here.

Eno. Humbly, sir, I thank you.

Exeunt.

[II. iii.] 8. **kept my square:** i.e., followed the straight and narrow path. A **square** is a footrule.

16-7. **see it in my motion, have it not in my tongue:** perceive it intuitively, but cannot explain it. **Motion** here means an "inward prompting."

18. **hie you:** hurry.

23. **daemon:** guardian spirit.

[Scene III. Rome. Cæsar's house.]

Enter Antony, Cæsar, Octavia between them.

Ant. The world, and my great office, will sometimes
Divide me from your bosom.
Octa. All which time
Before the gods my knee shall bow my prayers
To them for you.
Ant. Good night, sir. My Octavia,
Read not my blemishes in the world's report.
I have not kept my square; but that to come
Shall all be done by the rule. Good night, dear lady.
Octa. Good night, sir.
Cæs. Good night.

Exit [with Octavia].

Enter Soothsayer.

Ant. Now, sirrah, you do wish yourself in Egypt?
Sooth. Would I had never come from thence, nor you thither!
Ant. If you can, your reason!
Sooth. I see it in my motion, have it not in my tongue.
But yet hie you to Egypt again.
Ant. Say to me,
Whose fortunes shall rise higher, Cæsar's or mine?
Sooth. Cæsar's.
Therefore, O Antony, stay not by his side!
Thy daemon, that thy spirit which keeps thee, is

26. **afeard:** Thirlby's reading for the Folio "a fear."

31. **of:** because of.

32. **thickens:** dims.

40. **cunning:** skill.

41. **chance:** luck; **speeds:** prospers, wins.

42. **still:** always.

43. **it is all to naught:** i.e., the odds are all in my favor.

44. **inhooped:** encircled by a ring. English cock-fighting often took place in rings and Shakespeare has probably transferred this practice to the ancient sport of quailfighting popular in Rome.

Noble, courageous, high, unmatchable,
Where Cæsar's is not; but near him thy angel
Becomes afeard, as being o'erpow'red. Therefore
Make space enough between you.

Ant. Speak this no more.

Sooth. To none but thee; no more but when to thee.
If thou dost play with him at any game,
Thou art sure to lose; and of that natural luck
He beats thee 'gainst the odds. Thy luster thickens
When he shines by. I say again, thy spirit
Is all afraid to govern thee near him;
But he away, 'tis noble.

Ant. Get thee gone.
Say to Ventidius I would speak with him.

Exit [Soothsayer].

He shall to Parthia.—Be it art or hap,
He hath spoken true. The very dice obey him,
And in our sports my better cunning faints
Under his chance. If we draw lots, he speeds;
His cocks do win the battle still of mine
When it is all to naught, and his quails ever
Beat mine, inhooped, at odds. I will to Egypt;
And though I make this marriage for my peace,
I' the East my pleasure lies.

Enter Ventidius.

O, come, Ventidius,
You must to Parthia. Your commission's ready;
Follow me, and receive't.

Exeunt.

[II. iv.] 5. **e'en but:** merely.

9. **the Mount:** Mount Misenum; see [II. ii.] 202.

12. **much about:** out of the way, the long way around.

[II. v.] 1. **moody:** melancholy.

[Scene IV. Rome. A street.]

Enter Lepidus, Mæcenas, and Agrippa.

Lep. Trouble yourselves no further. Pray you, hasten
Your generals after.
Agr. Sir, Mark Antony
Will e'en but kiss Octavia, and we'll follow.
Lep. Till I shall see you in your soldier's dress,
Which will become you both, farewell.
Mæc. We shall,
As I conceive the journey, be at the Mount
Before you, Lepidus.
Lep. Your way is shorter;
My purposes do draw me much about.
You'll win two days upon me.
Both. Sir, good success!
Lep. Farewell.

Exeunt.

[Scene V. Alexandria. Cleopatra's Palace.]

Enter Cleopatra, Charmian, Iras, and Alexas.

Cleo. Give me some music! music, moody food
Of us that trade in love.
Omnes. The music, ho!

15. **Tawny-finned:** Theobald's correction of the Folio "tawny fine."

27. **tires:** headdresses.

28. **sword Philippan:** the sword that he used at the Battle of Philippi, where Brutus and Cassius were defeated.

Guillaume Du Choul, *Discours de la religion des anciens Romains* (1556)

Enter Mardian, the Eunuch.

Cleo. Let it alone! Let's to billiards. Come, Charmian.
Char. My arm is sore; best play with Mardian.
Cleo. As well a woman with an eunuch played
As with a woman. Come, you'll play with me, sir?
Mar. As well as I can, madam.
Cleo. And when good will is showed, though't come too short,
The actor may plead pardon. I'll none now.
Give me mine angle! we'll to the river. There,
My music playing far off, I will betray
Tawny-finned fishes. My bended hook shall pierce
Their slimy jaws; and as I draw them up,
I'll think them every one an Antony,
And say, "Ah, ha! y'are caught!"
Char. 'Twas merry when
You wagered on your angling, when your diver
Did hang a salt fish on his hook, which he
With fervency drew up.
Cleo. That time? O times!
I laughed him out of patience; and that night
I laughed him into patience; and next morn
Ere the ninth hour I drunk him to his bed,
Then put my tires and mantles on him, whilst
I wore his sword Philippan.

Enter a Messenger.

O, from Italy!
Ram thou thy fruitful tidings in mine ears,

35. **yield:** report.

47. **favor:** face, appearance.

49. **Fury:** one of the avenging deities of mythology.

50. **formal:** regular, according to the usual form.

54. **Or . . . or:** either . . . or.

That long time have been barren.
Mess. Madam, madam—
Cleo. Antony's dead! If thou say so, villain,
Thou killst thy mistress; but well and free,
If thou so yield him, there is gold, and here
My bluest veins to kiss—a hand that kings
Have lipped, and trembled kissing.
Mess. First, madam, he is well.
Cleo. Why, there's more gold.
But, sirrah, mark, we use
To say the dead are well. Bring it to that,
The gold I give thee will I melt and pour
Down thy ill-uttering throat.
Mess. Good madam, hear me.
Cleo. Well, go to, I will.
But there's no goodness in thy face. If Antony
Be free and healthful, why so tart a favor
To trumpet such good tidings? If not well,
Thou shouldst come like a Fury crowned with snakes,
Not like a formal man.
Mess. Will't please you hear me?
Cleo. I have a mind to strike thee ere thou speakst.
Yet, if thou say Antony lives, is well,
Or friends with Cæsar or not captive to him,
I'll set thee in a shower of gold and hail
Rich pearls upon thee.
Mess. Madam, he's well.
Cleo. Well said.
Mess. And friends with Cæsar.
Cleo. Th'art an honest man.
Mess. Cæsar and he are greater friends than ever.

64-5. **allay/The good precedence:** modify the preceding good news.

81. **spurn:** kick.

S.D. after l. 82. **hales:** pulls.

Cleo. Make thee a fortune from me!
Mess. But yet, madam—
Cleo. I do not like "but yet." It does allay
The good precedence. Fie upon "but yet"!
"But yet" is as a jailer to bring forth
Some monstrous malefactor. Prithee, friend,
Pour out the pack of matter to mine ear,
The good and bad together. He's friends with Cæsar;
In state of health thou sayst; and thou sayst free.
Mess. Free, madam? No; I made no such report.
He's bound unto Octavia.
Cleo. For what good turn?
Mess. For the best turn i' the bed.
Cleo. I am pale, Charmian.
Mess. Madam, he's married to Octavia.
Cleo. The most infectious pestilence upon thee!
Strikes him down.
Mess. Good madam, patience.
Cleo. What say you?
Strikes him.
Hence,
Horrible villain! or I'll spurn thine eyes
Like balls before me. I'll unhair thy head!
She hales him up and down.
Thou shalt be whipped with wire and stewed in brine,
Smarting in ling'ring pickle.
Mess. Gracious madam,
I that do bring the news made not the match.
Cleo. Say 'tis not so, a province I will give thee
And make thy fortunes proud. The blow thou hadst
Shall make thy peace for moving me to rage;

90. **boot thee with:** give thee in addition.

105-6. **I myself/Have given myself the cause:** i.e., my own folly in loving Antony is the cause of my distress at your news.

109. **gracious:** favorable.

110-11. **tell/Themselves when they be felt:** i.e., make themselves apparent when their consequences must be faced.

And I will boot thee with what gift beside
Thy modesty can beg.

Mess. He's married, madam.

Cleo. Rogue, thou hast lived too long. *Draw a knife.*

Mess. Nay, then I'll run.
What mean you, madam? I have made no fault. *Exit.*

Char. Good madam, keep yourself within yourself.
The man is innocent.

Cleo. Some innocents scape not the thunderbolt.
Melt Egypt into Nile! and kindly creatures
Turn all to serpents! Call the slave again.
Though I am mad, I will not bite him. Call!

Char. He is afeard to come.

Cleo. I will not hurt him.
These hands do lack nobility, that they strike
A meaner than myself; since I myself
Have given myself the cause.

Enter the Messenger again.

Come hither, sir.
Though it be honest, it is never good
To bring bad news. Give to a gracious message
An host of tongues, but let ill tidings tell
Themselves when they be felt.

Mess. I have done my duty.

Cleo. Is he married?
I cannot hate thee worser than I do
If thou again say yes.

Mess. He's married, madam.

117. **confound:** destroy.

121. **So:** even if.

123. **Narcissus:** a youth of Greek legend who was so beautiful that all the nymphs fell in love with him. Venus ultimately punished him for his pride by causing him to fall in love with his own image.

127. **Take no offense that I would not offend you:** i.e., do not be angry if at your request I repeat the news which offends you.

129. **unequal:** unjust.

131. **what th'art sure of:** that is, the fact of Antony's marriage. It is this which disturbs Cleopatra, and, in reason, she knows that the messenger is not at fault.

132. **merchandise:** commodities of trade, a plural, hence **Are** in l. 134.

134. **Lie they upon thy hand:** may you be unable to sell them.

143. **feature:** physical characteristics.

144. **inclination:** temperament.

Cleo. The gods confound thee! Dost thou hold there still?
Mess. Should I lie, madam?
Cleo. O, I would thou didst,
So half my Egypt were submerged and made
A cistern for scaled snakes! Go get thee hence!
Hadst thou Narcissus in thy face, to me
Thou wouldst appear most ugly. He is married?
Mess. I crave your Highness' pardon.
Cleo. He is married?
Mess. Take no offense that I would not offend you.
To punish me for what you make me do
Seems much unequal. He's married to Octavia.
Cleo. O, that his fault should make a knave of thee,
That art not what th'art sure of! Get thee hence.
The merchandise which thou hast brought from Rome
Are all too dear for me. Lie they upon thy hand,
And be undone by 'em! [*Exit Messenger.*]
Char. Good your Highness, patience.
Cleo. In praising Antony I have dispraised Cæsar.
Char. Many times, madam.
Cleo. I am paid for't now.
Lead me from hence,
I faint. O Iras, Charmian! 'Tis no matter.
Go to the fellow, good Alexas. Bid him
Report the feature of Octavia, her years,
Her inclination; let him not leave out
The color of her hair. Bring me word quickly.
[*Exit Alexas.*]
Let him forever go!—let him not!—Charmian,

147. **a Gorgon:** in Greek mythology, a woman with snakes instead of hair and so horrible in aspect that looking upon her face turned the beholder to stone.

[II. vi.] 3. **meet:** appropriate.

8. **tall:** brave.

12. **factors:** agents.

13. **want:** lack.

14-6. **since Julius Cæsar,/Who at Philippi the good Brutus ghosted,/There saw you laboring for him:** that is, since Julius Cæsar (to whom he compares his father) was avenged at Philippi by you.

Though he be painted one way like a Gorgon,
The other way's a Mars.—[*To Mardian*] Bid you Alexas
Bring me word how tall she is.—Pity me, Charmian,
But do not speak to me. Lead me to my chamber.
Exeunt.

[Scene VI. Near Misenum.]

Flourish. Enter Pompey at one door, with Drum and Trumpet: at another Cæsar, Lepidus, Antony, Enobarbus, Mæcenas, Agrippa, [*and*] *Menas with Soldiers marching.*

Pom. Your hostages I have, so have you mine;
And we shall talk before we fight.
Cæs. Most meet
That first we come to words; and therefore have we
Our written purposes before us sent;
Which if thou hast considered, let us know
If 'twill tie up thy discontented sword
And carry back to Sicily much tall youth
That else must perish here.
Pom. To you all three,
The senators alone of this great world,
Chief factors for the gods: I do not know
Wherefore my father should revengers want,
Having a son and friends, since Julius Cæsar,
Who at Philippi the good Brutus ghosted,
There saw you laboring for him. What was't

18. **honest:** honorable.

27. **fear:** frighten.

28. **speak with:** encounter.

29. **o'ercount:** outnumber.

31. **o'ercount me of my father's house:** when the house of Pompey the Great was put up for sale Antony bought it, but he later refused to pay the purchase price. **O'ercount** has a second sense of "cheat" here.

32. **the cuckoo:** a bird that lays its eggs in the nests of other birds instead of building its own.

35. **from the present:** beside the present point, irrelevant.

39. **embraced:** if accepted.

40-1. **what may follow,/To try a larger fortune:** the consequences of holding out for more than we have offered.

47. **targes:** targets; **undinted:** not marked with scars of battle.

That moved pale Cassius to conspire? and what
Made the all-honored honest Roman, Brutus,
With the armed rest, courtiers of beauteous freedom,
To drench the Capitol, but that they would
Have one man but a man? And that is it
Hath made me rig my navy, at whose burden
The angered ocean foams; with which I meant
To scourge the ingratitude that despiteful Rome
Cast on my noble father.

Cæs. Take your time.

Ant. Thou canst not fear us, Pompey, with thy sails.
We'll speak with thee at sea. At land thou knowst
How much we do o'ercount thee.

Pom. At land indeed
Thou dost o'ercount me of my father's house!
But since the cuckoo builds not for himself,
Remain in't as thou mayst.

Lep. Be pleased to tell us
(For this is from the present) how you take
The offers we have sent you.

Cæs. There's the point.

Ant. Which do not be entreated to, but weigh
What it is worth embraced.

Cæs. And what may follow,
To try a larger fortune.

Pom. You have made me offer
Of Sicily, Sardinia; and I must
Rid all the sea of pirates; then, to send
Measures of wheat to Rome; this 'greed upon,
To part with unhacked edges and bear back
Our targes undinted.

58. **studied:** prepared.

69. **What counts harsh Fortune casts upon my face:** that is, how my face reflects the harsh blows of Fortune. The metaphor is from keeping accounts by means of marks or scores.

74. **composition:** compact; see **compose** at [II.-ii.] 20.

Omnes. That's our offer.
Pom. Know then
I came before you here a man prepared
To take this offer; but Mark Antony
Put me to some impatience. Though I lose
The praise of it by telling, you must know,
When Cæsar and your brother were at blows,
Your mother came to Sicily and did find
Her welcome friendly.
Ant. I have heard it, Pompey,
And am well studied for a liberal thanks,
Which I do owe you.
Pom. Let me have your hand.
I did not think, sir, to have met you here.
Ant. The beds i' the East are soft; and thanks to you,
That called me timelier than my purpose hither;
For I have gained by't.
Cæs. Since I saw you last
There is a change upon you.
Pom. Well, I know not
What counts harsh Fortune casts upon my face;
But in my bosom shall she never come
To make my heart her vassal.
Lep. Well met here.
Pom. I hope so, Lepidus. Thus we are agreed.
I crave our composition may be written,
And sealed between us.
Cæs. That's the next to do.
Pom. We'll feast each other ere we part, and let's
Draw lots who shall begin.

88. **Apollodorus:** a Sicilian, reported by Plutarch to have carried Cleopatra into Cæsar's presence wrapped in a mattress.

95. **toward:** impending.

Ant. That will I, Pompey.
Pom. No, Antony, take the lot;
But, first or last, your fine Egyptian cookery
Shall have the fame. I have heard that Julius Cæsar
Grew fat with feasting there.
Ant. You have heard much.
Pom. I have fair meanings, sir.
Ant. And fair words to them.
Pom. Then so much have I heard;
And I have heard Apollodorus carried—
Eno. No more of that! He did so.
Pom. What, I pray you?
Eno. A certain queen to Cæsar in a mattress.
Pom. I know thee now. How farest thou, soldier?
Eno. Well;
And well am like to do, for I perceive
Four feasts are toward.
Pom. Let me shake thy hand.
I never hated thee. I have seen thee fight
When I have envied thy behavior.
Eno. Sir,
I never loved you much; but I ha' praised ye
When you have well deserved ten times as much
As I have said you did.
Pom. Enjoy thy plainness;
It nothing ill becomes thee.
Aboard my galley I invite you all.
Will you lead, lords?
All. Show us the way, sir.
Pom. Come.
Exeunt. Manent Enobarbus and Menas.

122. **authority:** that is, to make arrests.
124. **true:** honest.
134. **Y'have said:** you have spoken truly.

Caius Marcellus—Jacobus de Strada, *Epitome thesauri antiquitatum* (1557)

Menas. [*Aside*] Thy father, Pompey, would ne'er have made this treaty.—You and I have known, sir.

Eno. At sea, I think.

Menas. We have, sir.

Eno. You have done well by water.

Menas. And you by land.

Eno. I will praise any man that will praise me; though it cannot be denied what I have done by land.

Menas. Nor what I have done by water.

Eno. Yes, something you can deny for your own safety. You have been a great thief by sea.

Menas. And you by land.

Eno. There I deny my land service. But give me your hand, Menas. If our eyes had authority, here they might take two thieves kissing.

Menas. All men's faces are true, whatsome'er their hands are.

Eno. But there is never a fair woman has a true face.

Menas. No slander. They steal hearts.

Eno. We came hither to fight with you.

Menas. For my part, I am sorry it is turned to a drinking. Pompey doth this day laugh away his fortune.

Eno. If he do, sure he cannot weep't back again.

Menas. Y'have said, sir. We looked not for Mark Antony here. Pray you, is he married to Cleopatra?

Eno. Cæsar's sister is called Octavia.

Menas. True, sir. She was the wife of Caius Marcellus.

Eno. But she is now the wife of Marcus Antonius.

145-46. **made more in:** contributed more to.

147. **band:** bond.

150. **conversation:** manner of life.

157. **use his affection where it is:** continue to seek love where he has in the past (with Cleopatra).

158. **occasion:** advantage.

Menas. Pray ye, sir?

Eno. 'Tis true.

Menas. Then is Cæsar and he forever knit together.

Eno. If I were bound to divine of this unity, I would not prophesy so.

Menas. I think the policy of that purpose made more in the marriage than the love of the parties.

Eno. I think so too. But you shall find the band that seems to tie their friendship together will be the very strangler of their amity. Octavia is of a holy, cold, and still conversation.

Menas. Who would not have his wife so?

Eno. Not he that himself is not so; which is Mark Antony. He will to his Egyptian dish again. Then shall the sighs of Octavia blow the fire up in Cæsar, and, as I said before, that which is the strength of their amity shall prove the immediate author of their variance. Antony will use his affection where it is. He married but his occasion here.

Menas. And thus it may be. Come, sir, will you aboard? I have a health for you.

Eno. I shall take it, sir. We have used our throats in Egypt.

Menas. Come, let's away.

Exeunt.

[II. vii.] 1. **plants:** a pun. **Plants** has a second meaning "feet." The company has been drinking heavily and are now unsteady on their feet.

5. **alms drink:** that portion of the drink which would normally be reserved for the poor; in this case, probably, more than his share.

6-8. **As they pinch one another by the disposition, he cries out "No more!" reconciles them to his entreaty and himself to the drink:** that is, as their dispositions begin to clash, he intervenes to restore peace and, having succeeded, has another drink.

13. **partisan:** long-handled weapon.

14-6. **To be called into a huge sphere and not to be seen to move in't, are the holes where eyes should be, which pitifully disaster the cheeks:** to have the opportunity of mingling with the great and be unable to distinguish oneself among them is as unfortunate as having only blank holes where one's eyes should be. **Disaster** is an astrological term for an ill omen.

S.D. after l. 16. **sennet:** a series of trumpet notes.

21. **foison:** abundance.

[Scene VII. On board Pompey's galley, off Misenum.]

Music plays. Enter two or three Servants, with a banquet.

1. Serv. Here they'll be, man. Some o' their plants are ill-rooted already; the least wind i' the world will blow them down.

2. Serv. Lepidus is high-colored.

1. Serv. They have made him drink alms drink.

2. Serv. As they pinch one another by the disposition, he cries out "No more!" reconciles them to his entreaty and himself to the drink.

1. Serv. But it raises the greater war between him and his discretion.

2. Serv. Why, this it is to have a name in great men's fellowship. I had as lief have a reed that will do me no service as a partisan I could not heave.

1. Serv. To be called into a huge sphere and not to be seen to move in't, are the holes where eyes should be, which pitifully disaster the cheeks.

A sennet sounded. Enter Cæsar, Antony, Pompey, Lepidus, Agrippa, Mæcenas, Enobarbus, Menas, with other Captains.

Ant. [*To Cæsar*] Thus do they, sir: they take the flow o' the Nile
By certain scales i' the pyramid. They know
By the height, the lowness, or the mean, if dearth
Or foison follow. The higher Nilus swells,

32. **out:** i.e., pass out.

33. **in:** i.e., in liquor, drunk.

36. **pyramises:** pyramids. The original Latin spelling *pyramis* was the usual singular form of the word; the plural usually appeared as "pyramides."

49. **it:** its.

50. **the elements:** the vital elements, earth, air, fire, and water, which contemporary physical science considered the components of life.

The personification of the Nile—Vincenzo Cartari, *Imagini de gli dei delli antichi* (1615)

The more it promises. As it ebbs, the seedsman
Upon the slime and ooze scatters his grain,
And shortly comes to harvest.

Lep. Y'have strange serpents there.

Ant. Ay, Lepidus.

Lep. Your serpent of Egypt is bred now of your mud by the operation of your sun; so is your crocodile.

Ant. They are so.

Pom. Sit—and some wine! A health to Lepidus!

Lep. I am not so well as I should be, but I'll ne'er out.

Eno. Not till you have slept. I fear me you'll be in till then.

Lep. Nay, certainly, I have heard the Ptolemies' pyramises are very goodly things. Without contradiction I have heard that.

Menas. [*Aside to Pompey*] Pompey, a word.

Pom. [*Aside to Menas*] Say in mine ear.
What is't?

Menas. [*Aside to Pompey*] Forsake thy seat, I do beseech thee, Captain,
And hear me speak a word.

Pom. [*Aside to Menas*] Forbear me till anon.
Whispers in's ear.
This wine for Lepidus!

Lep. What manner o' thing is your crocodile?

Ant. It is shaped, sir, like itself, and it is as broad as it hath breadth. It is just so high as it is, and moves with it own organs. It lives by that which nourisheth it, and the elements once out of it, it transmigrates.

Lep. What color is it of?

66. **held my cap off to:** deferred to, served.

70-1. **These quicksands, Lepidus,/Keep off them, for you sink:** Lepidus has exceeded his capacity and now sinks into a stupor.

77. **entertain it:** receive the idea favorably.

Nile crocodile—Pierre Belon, *Observations de plusieurs singularitez* (1588)

Ant. Of it own color too.
Lep. 'Tis a strange serpent.
Ant. 'Tis so. And the tears of it are wet.
Cæs. Will this description satisfy him?
Ant. With the health that Pompey gives him; else he is a very epicure.
Pom. [*Aside to Menas*] Go hang, sir, hang! Tell me of that? Away!
Do as I bid you.—Where's this cup I called for?
Menas. [*Aside to Pompey*] If for the sake of merit thou wilt hear me,
Rise from thy stool.
Pom. [*Aside to Menas*] I think th'art mad.
[*Rises and walks aside.*]
The matter?
Menas. I have ever held my cap off to thy fortunes.
Pom. Thou hast served me with much faith. What's else to say?—
Be jolly, lords.
Ant. These quicksands, Lepidus,
Keep off them, for you sink.
Menas. Wilt thou be lord of all the world?
Pom. What sayst thou?
Menas. Wilt thou be lord of the whole world? That's twice.
Pom. How should that be?
Menas. But entertain it,
And though thou think me poor, I am the man
Will give thee all the world.
Pom. Hast thou drunk well?
Menas. No, Pompey, I have kept me from the cup.

83. **pales:** hems in, encloses; **inclips:** embraces.

86-7. **competitors:** partners; see I. [iv.] 3.

100. **palled:** weakened, dimmed. Menas feels that the present moment is a turning point in Pompey's career and that, having failed to take advantage of the opportunity to rid himself of rivals, his fortunes can only decline.

110. **'A:** he.

Thou art, if thou darest be, the earthly Jove.
Whate'er the ocean pales, or sky inclips,
Is thine, if thou wilt ha't.

Pom. Show me which way.

Menas. These three world-sharers, these competitors,
Are in thy vessel. Let me cut the cable;
And when we are put off, fall to their throats.
All there is thine.

Pom. Ah, this thou shouldst have done,
And not have spoke on't! In me 'tis villainy;
In thee't had been good service. Thou must know,
'Tis not my profit that does lead mine honor;
Mine honor, it. Repent that e'er thy tongue
Hath so betrayed thine act. Being done unknown,
I should have found it afterwards well done,
But must condemn it now. Desist, and drink.

Menas. [*Aside*] For this,
I'll never follow thy palled fortunes more.
Who seeks, and will not take when once 'tis offered,
Shall never find it more.

Pom. This health to Lepidus!

Ant. Bear him ashore. I'll pledge it for him, Pompey.

Eno. Here's to thee, Menas!

Menas. Enobarbus, welcome!

Pom. Fill till the cup be hid.

Eno. There's a strong fellow, Menas.
[*Points to the Servant who carries off Lepidus.*]

Menas. Why?

Eno. 'A bears the third part of the world, man; seest not?

114. **go on wheels:** i.e., move speedily, a reference to the proverbial saying "The world runs on wheels," meaning that everything is going well.

115. **Increase the reels:** add to the number of those reeling and thus to the likelihood of the whole world's doing so.

118. **Strike the vessels:** a nautical term meaning to empty a vessel of its load—"everybody drink up."

121. **monstrous:** outrageously absurd.

124. **Possess it; I'll make answer:** drink up your toast; I'll drink in answer.

132. **Till that:** until.

133. **Lethe:** forgetfulness; see note at [II. i.] 33.

137. **holding:** burden, refrain.

Menas. The third part, then, is drunk. Would it were all,
That it might go on wheels!
Eno. Drink thou. Increase the reels.
Menas. Come.
Pom. This is not yet an Alexandrian feast.
Ant. It ripens towards it. Strike the vessels, ho!
Here's to Cæsar!
Cæs. I could well forbear't.
It's monstrous labor when I wash my brain
And it grows fouler.
Ant. Be a child o' the time.
Cæs. Possess it; I'll make answer.
But I had rather fast from all four days
Than drink so much in one.
Eno. [*To Antony*] Ha, my brave emperor!
Shall we dance now the Egyptian Bacchanals
And celebrate our drink?
Pom. Let's ha't, good soldier.
Ant. Come, let's all take hands
Till that the conquering wine hath steeped our sense
In soft and delicate Lethe.
Eno. All take hands.
Make battery to our ears with the loud music,
The while I'll place you; then the boy shall sing.
The holding every man shall bear as loud
As his strong sides can volley.

140. **Plumpy Bacchus with pink eyne:** plump Bacchus (god of wine) with pink (blinking) eyes.

141. **fats:** vats.

147. **off:** that is, to come with me.

151-52. **The wild disguise hath almost/Anticked us all:** we are all so affected by our drinking that we have almost turned into buffoons.

154. **try you on the shore:** vie with you in drinking on shore.

155. **And shall:** agreed!

Music plays. Enobarbus places them hand in hand.

The Song.

Come, thou monarch of the vine,
Plumpy Bacchus with pink eyne!
In thy fats our cares be drowned,
With thy grapes our hairs be crowned.
Cup us till the world go round,
Cup us till the world go round!

Cæs. What would you more? Pompey, good night.
Good brother,
Let me request you off. Our graver business
Frowns at this levity. Gentle lords, let's part;
You see we have burnt our cheeks. Strong Enobarb
Is weaker than the wine, and mine own tongue
Splits what it speaks. The wild disguise hath almost
Anticked us all. What needs more words? Good night.
Good Antony, your hand.

Pom. I'll try you on the shore.

Ant. And shall, sir.—Give's your hand.

Pom. O Antony,
You have my father's house—but what? We are friends!
Come, down into the boat.

Eno. Take heed you fall not.

[*Exeunt all but Enobarbus and Menas.*]

Menas, I'll not on shore.

167. **Hoo! says 'a. There's my cap:** a mocking shout in honor of the departing "great fellows," throwing his hat in the air.

Pacorus of Parthia—Guillaume Rouillé, *Promptuarii iconum* (1553)
(See III. i. 5.)

Menas. No, to my cabin.
These drums! these trumpets, flutes! what!
Let Neptune hear we bid a loud farewell
To these great fellows. Sound and be hanged, sound out!

Sound a flourish, with drums.

Eno. Hoo! says' a. There's my cap.

Menas. Hoo! Noble Captain, come.

Exeunt.

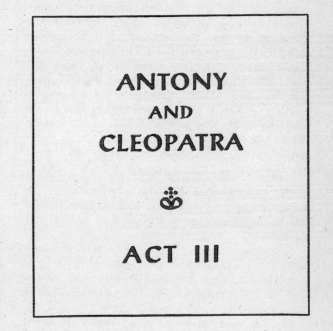

ANTONY AND CLEOPATRA

ACT III

[III.] The reconciliation between the triumvirs and Pompey is not of long duration. Cæsar is also soon at odds with Antony and when Octavia leaves for Rome to intercede in Antony's behalf he returns to Cleopatra. In the meantime Cæsar has fought and defeated Pompey and arrested Lepidus on charges of conspiracy. He is displeased with Antony for wronging his sister and bestowing kingdoms on Cleopatra's children. War between Cæsar and Antony follows. Ignoring his friends' advice, Antony meets Cæsar at sea near Actium, and when Cleopatra's ship flees the battle he follows. The victorious Cæsar shows himself implacable toward Antony but is disposed to be charitable to Cleopatra if she will abandon her lover. With Cleopatra's encouragement, however, Antony is heartened enough to fight Cæsar again by land. The faithful Enobarbus, observing the decline of Antony's judgment and valor, is pessimistic and begins to think of deserting him.

[III. i.] 1. **darting Parthia:** a reference to the famed skill of the Parthians in wielding darts as missiles in battle; **stroke:** struck (as if by one of your own darts).

3. **Marcus Crassus:** a member of the first triumvirate, who was killed by the Parthians.

5. **Orodes:** King of Parthia. **Pacorus** was his son.

9. **Media:** a country in Asia Minor surrounded by Armenia, Persia, Parthia, and Hyrcania.

15-6. **A lower place . . ./May make too great an act:** i.e., men of lower rank should not compete with their leaders in performing spectacular feats.

[*ACT III*]

[Scene I. A plain in Syria.]

Enter Ventidius as it were in triumph, [with Silius and other Romans, Officers, and Soldiers;] the dead body of Pacorus borne before him.

Ven. Now, darting Parthia, art thou stroke, and now
Pleased fortune does of Marcus Crassus' death
Make me revenger. Bear the King's son's body
Before our army. Thy Pacorus, Orodes,
Pays this for Marcus Crassus.
Silius. Noble Ventidius,
Whilst yet with Parthian blood thy sword is warm,
The fugitive Parthians follow. Spur through Media,
Mesopotamia, and the shelters whither
The routed fly. So thy grand captain, Antony,
Shall set thee on triumphant chariots and
Put garlands on thy head.
Ven. O Silius, Silius,
I have done enough. A lower place, note well,
May make too great an act. For learn this, Silius:
Better to leave undone than by our deed
Acquire too high a fame when him we serve's away.
Cæsar and Antony have ever won
More in their officer than person. Sossius,

21. **his:** i.e., Antony's.

26-7. **rather makes choice of loss/Than gain which darkens him:** i.e., would rather forfeit personal glory than incur his commander's displeasure by overshadowing him.

31-3. **Thou hast . . . that/Without the which a soldier and his sword/Grants scarce distinction:** you have wisdom; a soldier who lacks it is a mere tool of battle.

37. **horse:** cavalry.

38. **jaded out o' the field:** routed, as though the horses were jades (nags).

[**III. ii.**] 1. **brothers:** brothers-in-law (Cæsar and Antony).

Roman archer—Guillaume Du Choul, *Discours de la religion des anciens Romains* (1556)

One of my place in Syria, his lieutenant,
For quick accumulation of renown,
Which he achieved by the minute, lost his favor.
Who does i' the wars more than his captain can
Becomes his captain's captain; and ambition,
The soldier's virtue, rather makes choice of loss
Than gain which darkens him.
I could do more to do Antonius good,
But 'twould offend him; and in his offense
Should my performance perish.

Silius. Thou hast, Ventidius, that
Without the which a soldier and his sword
Grants scarce distinction. Thou wilt write to Antony?

Ven. I'll humbly signify what in his name,
That magical word of war, we have effected;
How with his banners and his well-paid ranks
The ne'er-yet-beaten horse of Parthia
We have jaded out o' the field.

Silius. Where is he now?

Ven. He purposeth to Athens; whither, with what haste
The weight we must convey with 's will permit,
We shall appear before him.—On, there! Pass along!

Exeunt.

[Scene II. Rome. Cæsar's house.]

Enter Agrippa at one door, Enobarbus at another.

Agr. What, are the brothers parted?

Eno. They have dispatched with Pompey; he is gone;

4. **sealing:** signing their agreement.

7. **greensickness:** an anemia usually associated with lovesick young girls. Enobarbus is being ironic throughout.

14. **Arabian bird:** phoenix, a legendary bird believed to inhabit Arabia, used here as the epitome of rarity because only one phoenix ever existed at a time.

26. **They are his shards, and he their beetle: shard** means a piece of cow dung; the beetle referred to is the tumblebug, which lives and breeds in dung.

30. **No further:** please do not trouble to escort me further.

The other three are sealing. Octavia weeps
To part from Rome; Cæsar is sad; and Lepidus
Since Pompey's feast, as Menas says, is troubled
With the greensickness.
Agr. 'Tis a noble Lepidus.
Eno. A very fine one. O, how he loves Cæsar!
Agr. Nay, but how dearly he adores Mark Antony!
Eno. Cæsar? Why, he's the Jupiter of men.
Agr. What's Antony? The god of Jupiter.
Eno. Spake you of Cæsar? Hoo! the nonpareil!
Agr. O Antony! O thou Arabian bird!
Eno. Would you praise Cæsar, say "Cæsar"—go no further.
Agr. Indeed he plied them both with excellent praises.
Eno. But he loves Cæsar best. Yet he loves Antony!
Hoo! hearts, tongues, figures, scribes, bards, poets, cannot
Think, speak, cast, write, sing, number—hoo!—
His love to Antony. But as for Cæsar,
Kneel down, kneel down, and wonder!
Agr. Both he loves.
Eno. They are his shards, and he their beetle. [*Trumpet within.*] So:
This is to horse. Adieu, noble Agrippa.
Agr. Good fortune, worthy soldier, and farewell!

Enter Cæsar, Antony, Lepidus, and Octavia.

Ant. No further, sir.
Cæs. You take from me a great part of myself;

33-4. **as my farthest band/Shall pass on thy approof:** as I would be willing to stake my uttermost that you will prove.

35. **piece:** unique example, masterpiece.

43. **I have said:** I will say no more.

45. **curious:** unusually particular or careful in examination.

50. **elements:** heavens.

53-4. **The April's in her eyes. It is love's spring,/And these the showers to bring it on:** she weeps. Her love is young and tears will nourish it.

59-62. **Her tongue will not obey her heart, nor can/Her heart inform her tongue—the swan's-down feather/That stands upon the swell at full of tide,/And neither way inclines:** she cannot express her mixed emotions at parting with her brother and going to live with Antony; she wavers between the two feelings like a feather balancing on the water between tides.

Use me well in't. Sister, prove such a wife
As my thoughts make thee, and as my farthest band
Shall pass on thy approof. Most noble Antony,
Let not the piece of virtue which is set
Betwixt us as the cement of our love
To keep it builded, be the ram to batter
The fortress of it; for better might we
Have loved without this mean, if on both parts
This be not cherished.
Ant. Make me not offended
In your distrust.
Cæs. I have said.
Ant. You shall not find,
Though you be therein curious, the least cause
For what you seem to fear. So the gods keep you
And make the hearts of Romans serve your ends!
We will here part.
Cæs. Farewell, my dearest sister, fare thee well.
The elements be kind to thee and make
Thy spirits all of comfort! Fare thee well.
Octa. My noble brother!
Ant. The April's in her eyes. It is love's spring,
And these the showers to bring it on. Be cheerful.
Octa. Sir, look well to my husband's house; and—
Cæs. What,
Octavia?
Octa. I'll tell you in your ear.
Ant. Her tongue will not obey her heart, nor can
Her heart inform her tongue—the swan's-down feather
That stands upon the swell at full of tide,
And neither way inclines.

73. **rheum:** head cold.

74. **confound:** destroy, as at [II. v.] 117.

77-8. **still:** ever; **The time shall not/Outgo my thinking on you:** i.e., I shall think of you every minute.

80. **I'll wrestle with you in my strength of love:** I'll demonstrate the strength of my love by this embrace.

Eno. [*Aside to Agrippa*] Will Cæsar weep?

Agr. [*Aside to Enobarbus*] He has a cloud in's face.

Eno. [*Aside to Agrippa*] He were the worse for that, were he a horse;
So is he, being a man.

Agr. [*Aside to Enobarbus*] Why, Enobarbus,
When Antony found Julius Cæsar dead,
He cried almost to roaring; and he wept
When at Philippi he found Brutus slain.

Eno. [*Aside to Agrippa*] That year indeed he was troubled with a rheum.
What willingly he did confound he wailed,
Believe't, till I wept too.

Cæs. No, sweet Octavia,
You shall hear from me still. The time shall not
Outgo my thinking on you.

Ant. Come, sir, come.
I'll wrestle with you in my strength of love.
Look, here I have you; thus I let you go,
And give you to the gods.

Cæs. Adieu, be happy!

Lep. Let all the number of the stars give light
To thy fair way!

Cæs. Farewell, farewell! *Kisses Octavia.*

Ant. Farewell!

Trumpets sound. Exeunt.

Herod—Guillaume Rouillé, *Promptuarii iconum* (1553)

[Scene III. Alexandria. Cleopatra's Palace.]

Enter Cleopatra, Charmian, Iras, and Alexas.

Cleo. Where is the fellow?
Alex. Half afeard to come.
Cleo. Go to, go to!

Enter the Messenger, as before.

Come hither, sir.
Alex. Good Majesty,
Herod of Jewry dare not look upon you
But when you are well pleased.
Cleo. That Herod's head
I'll have! But how, when Antony is gone
Through whom I might command it? Come thou near.
Mess. Most gracious Majesty!
Cleo. Didst thou behold Octavia?
Mess. Ay, dread Queen.
Cleo. Where?
Mess. Madam, in Rome.
I looked her in the face, and saw her led
Between her brother and Mark Antony.
Cleo. Is she as tall as me?
Mess. She is not, madam.
Cleo. Didst hear her speak? Is she shrill-tongued or low?
Mess. Madam, I heard her speak. She is low-voiced.
Cleo. That's not so good! He cannot like her long.

[III. iii.] 30. **Her motion and her station are as one:** i.e., one can hardly tell whether she is moving or standing still.

31. **shows:** appears.

53. **As low as she would wish it:** i.e., her forehead is already so low as to be a defect.

Char. Like her? O Isis! 'tis impossible.
Cleo. I think so, Charmian. Dull of tongue, and dwarfish!
What majesty is in her gait? Remember,
If e'er thou lookst on majesty.
Mess. She creeps!
Her motion and her station are as one.
She shows a body rather than a life,
A statue than a breather.
Cleo. Is this certain?
Mess. Or I have no observance.
Char. Three in Egypt
Cannot make better note.
Cleo. He's very knowing;
I do perceive't. There's nothing in her yet.
The fellow has good judgment.
Char. Excellent.
Cleo. Guess at her years, I prithee.
Mess. Madam,
She was a widow—
Cleo. Widow? Charmian, hark!
Mess. And I do think she's thirty.
Cleo. Bear'st thou her face in mind? Is't long or round?
Mess. Round even to faultiness.
Cleo. For the most part, too, they are foolish that are so.
Her hair, what color?
Mess. Brown, madam; and her forehead
As low as she would wish it.

59. **proper:** excellent.
62. **no such thing:** nothing much.
66. **defend:** forbid.

[III. iv.] 3. **semblable:** similar.

Cleo. There's gold for thee.
Thou must not take my former sharpness ill.
I will employ thee back again; I find thee
Most fit for business. Go, make thee ready;
Our letters are prepared.

[*Exit Messenger.*]

Char. A proper man.

Cleo. Indeed he is so. I repent me much
That so I harried him. Why, methinks, by him,
This creature's no such thing.

Char. Nothing, madam.

Cleo. The man hath seen some majesty, and should know.

Char. Hath he seen majesty? Isis else defend,
And serving you so long!

Cleo. I have one thing more to ask him yet, good Charmian.
But 'tis no matter. Thou shalt bring him to me
Where I will write. All may be well enough.

Char. I warrant you, madam.

Exeunt.

[Scene IV. Athens. Antony's house.]

Enter Antony and Octavia.

Ant. Nay, nay, Octavia; not only that—
That were excusable, that and thousands more
Of semblable import—but he hath waged

6-7. **when perforce he could not/But:** when he had no choice but to.

8. **vented:** uttered.

9-10. **hint:** opportunity; **he not took't,/Or did it from his teeth:** he let the opportunity pass or praised Antony grudgingly.

13. **Stomach:** resent; see [II. ii.] 11.

16. **presently:** immediately.

26. **branchless:** unadorned, having been pruned of honor.

29. **stain:** overshadow, eclipse.

30. **So your desires are yours:** i.e., your speedy intervention will be needed if peace is to prevail between Cæsar and myself.

New wars 'gainst Pompey; made his will, and read it
To public ear;
Spoke scantly of me: when perforce he could not
But pay me terms of honor, cold and sickly
He vented them, most narrow measure lent me;
When the best hint was given him, he not took't,
Or did it from his teeth.

Octa. O, my good lord,
Believe not all; or if you must believe,
Stomach not all. A more unhappy lady,
If this division chance, ne'er stood between,
Praying for both parts.
The good gods will mock me presently
When I shall pray "O, bless my lord and husband!"
Undo that prayer by crying out as loud
"O, bless my brother!" Husband win, win brother,
Prays, and destroys the prayer; no midway
'Twixt these extremes at all.

Ant. Gentle Octavia,
Let your best love draw to that point which seeks
Best to preserve it. If I lose mine honor,
I lose myself. Better I were not yours
Than yours so branchless. But, as you requested,
Yourself shall go between's. The meantime, lady,
I'll raise the preparation of a war
Shall stain your brother. Make your soonest haste;
So your desires are yours.

Octa. Thanks to my lord.
The Jove of power make me most weak, most weak,
Your reconciler! Wars 'twixt you twain would be

36. where this begins: the origin of this rift.

[III. v.] 6. success: result.

8. **rivality:** equality with himself.

11. **appeal:** accusation.

12. **up:** confined, in custody.

13-6. **Then, world, thou hast a pair of chaps, no more;/And throw between them all the food thou hast,/They'll grind the one the other:** then there are only two pair of jaws in the world, Cæsar and Antony, and they are so voracious that no amount of food will keep them from devouring each other. The Folio reads "would," for which Hanmer supplied "world."

As if the world should cleave, and that slain men
Should solder up the rift.

Ant. When it appears to you where this begins,
Turn your displeasure that way, for our faults
Can never be so equal that your love
Can equally move with them. Provide your going;
Choose your own company, and command what cost
Your heart has mind to.

Exeunt.

[Scene V. Athens. Another room in Antony's house.]

Enter Enobarbus and Eros.

Eno. How now, friend Eros?

Eros. There's strange news come, sir.

Eno. What, man?

Eros. Cæsar and Lepidus have made wars upon Pompey.

Eno. This is old. What is the success?

Eros. Cæsar, having made use of him in the wars 'gainst Pompey, presently denied him rivality, would not let him partake in the glory of the action; and not resting here, accuses him of letters he had formerly wrote to Pompey; upon his own appeal, seizes him. So the poor third is up till death enlarge his confine.

Eno. Then, world, thou hast a pair of chaps, no more;
And throw between them all the food thou hast,
They'll grind the one the other. Where's Antony?

17. **spurns:** kicks at; see [II. v.] 81.

19. **that his officer:** that officer of his own.

20. **murd'red Pompey:** after a naval defeat at the hands of Agrippa, the fleeing Pompey was captured by Antony's forces and killed. Plutarch gives the name of his actual executioner as Titius, one of Antony's lieutenants.

22. **Domitius:** Enobarbus' given name.

25-6. **'Twill be naught;/But let it be:** i.e., the expedition will come to naught; but let's not dwell on the matter.

[III. vi.] 4. **tribunal:** raised platform.

7. **my father's son:** i.e., the son of Julius Cæsar, of whom Octavius himself was an adopted child. Cæsarion was the son of Cleopatra and Julius Cæsar.

10. **stablishment:** government.

Eros. He's walking in the garden thus, and spurns
The rush that lies before him; cries "Fool Lepidus!"
And threats the throat of that his officer
That murd'red Pompey.

Eno. Our great navy's rigged.

Eros. For Italy and Cæsar. More, Domitius:
My lord desires you presently. My news
I might have told hereafter.

Eno. 'Twill be naught;
But let it be. Bring me to Antony.

Eros. Come, sir.

Exeunt.

[Scene VI. Rome. Cæsar's house.]

Enter Agrippa, Mæcenas, and Cæsar.

Cæs. Contemning Rome, he has done all this and more
In Alexandria. Here's the manner of't:
I' the market place on a tribunal silvered
Cleopatra and himself in chairs of gold
Were publicly enthroned. At the feet sat
Cæsarion, whom they call my father's son,
And all the unlawful issue that their lust
Since then hath made between them. Unto her
He gave the stablishment of Egypt; made her
Of lower Syria, Cyprus, Lydia,
Absolute queen.

Mæc. This in the public eye?

19. **Cilicia:** a country on the seacoast of Asia Minor north of Cyprus.

20. **habiliments:** vestments, attire.

30. **spoiled:** looted; **rated:** allotted.

The goddess Isis—Vincenzo Cartari, *Imagini de gli dei delli antichi* (1615)

Cæs. I' the common show place, where they exercise.
His sons he there proclaimed the kings of kings:
Great Media, Parthia, and Armenia
He gave to Alexander; to Ptolemy he assigned
Syria, Cilicia, and Phoenicia. She
In the habiliments of the goddess Isis
That day appeared; and oft before gave audience,
As 'tis reported, so.

Mæc. Let Rome be thus informed.

Agr. Who, queasy with his insolence
Already, will their good thoughts call from him.

Cæs. The people know it, and have now received
His accusations.

Agr. Who does he accuse?

Cæs. Cæsar; and that, having in Sicily
Sextus Pompeius spoiled, we had not rated him
His part o' the isle. Then does he say he lent me
Some shipping unrestored. Lastly, he frets
That Lepidus of the triumvirate
Should be deposed; and, being, that we detain
All his revenue.

Agr. Sir, this should be answered.

Cæs. 'Tis done already, and the messenger gone.
I have told him Lepidus was grown too cruel,
That he his high authority abused
And did deserve his change. For what I have conquered,
I grant him part; but then in his Armenia,
And other of his conquered kingdoms, I
Demand the like.

63-4. **ostentation:** display; **which, left unshown, /Is often left unloved:** i.e., love which is not displayed often ceases to be felt; **should:** i.e., would.

Mæc. He'll never yield to that.
Cæs. Nor must not then be yielded to in this.

Enter Octavia with her Train.

Octa. Hail, Cæsar, and my lord! hail, most dear Cæsar!
Cæs. That ever I should call thee castaway!
Octa. You have not called me so, nor have you cause.
Cæs. Why have you stol'n upon us thus? You come not
Like Cæsar's sister. The wife of Antony
Should have an army for an usher, and
The neighs of horse to tell of her approach
Long ere she did appear. The trees by the way
Should have borne men, and expectation fainted,
Longing for what it had not. Nay, the dust
Should have ascended to the roof of heaven,
Raised by your populous troops. But you are come
A market-maid to Rome, and have prevented
The ostentation of our love, which, left unshown,
Is often left unloved. We should have met you
By sea and land, supplying every stage
With an augmented greeting.
Octa. Good my lord,
To come thus was I not constrained, but did it
On my free will. My lord, Mark Antony,
Hearing that you prepared for war, acquainted
My grieved ear withal; whereon I begged
His pardon for return.

74. **Being an abstract 'tween his lust and him:** Shakespeare has apparently made a noun out of one of the verbal senses of abstract. Octavia's return to Rome is a removal that will make it easier for Antony to depart for Egypt and Cleopatra.

82. **who now are:** i.e., Cleopatra and Antony; **levying:** mustering, calling up.

84. **Libya:** the ancient name for Africa.

85. **Cappadocia:** a country in Asia Minor northeast of Cilicia.

86. **Paphlagonia:** a country next to Cappadocia.

87. **Pont:** Pontus, a kingdom near Armenia.

89. **Comagene:** a part of Syria above Cilicia.

90. **Lycaonia:** a country southeast of Cappadocia.

97. **wronged:** suggested by Edward Capell for "wrong led" in the Folio.

98. **in negligent danger:** endangered by failure to take action.

100. **content:** happiness.

101. **determined things to destiny:** i.e., things which destiny has already determined, predetermined things.

Mithridates—Guillaume Rouillé, *Promptuarii iconum* (1553)

Cæs. Which soon he granted,
Being an abstract 'tween his lust and him.
Octa. Do not say so, my lord.
Cæs. I have eyes upon him,
And his affairs come to me on the wind.
Where is he now?
Octa. My lord, in Athens.
Cæs. No, my most wronged sister. Cleopatra
Hath nodded him to her. He hath given his empire
Up to a whore, who now are levying
The kings o' the earth for war. He hath assembled
Bocchus, the king of Libya; Archelaus,
Of Cappadocia; Philadelphos, king
Of Paphlagonia; the Thracian king, Adallas;
King Malchus of Arabia; King of Pont;
Herod of Jewry; Mithridates, king
Of Comagene; Polemon and Amyntas,
The kings of Mede and Lycaonia, with a
More larger list of scepters.
Octa. Ay me most wretched,
That have my heart parted betwixt two friends
That do afflict each other!
Cæs. Welcome hither.
Your letters did withhold our breaking forth,
Till we perceived both how you were wronged
And we in negligent danger. Cheer your heart!
Be you not troubled with the time, which drives
O'er your content these strong necessities;
But let determined things to destiny
Hold unbewailed their way. Welcome to Rome,
Nothing more dear to me! You are abused

104. **mark:** boundary, limit.

105. **make them ministers:** make agents for themselves.

111. **large:** free and open.

113. **regiment:** rule; **trull:** whore.

114. **noises it:** creates disturbances.

117. **known to patience:** acquainted with patience, patient.

[III. vii.] Setting. **Actium:** a promontory in southwestern Greece.

---

3. **forspoke:** spoken against.

6. **If not, denounced against us:** even if it is not fit, since war has been declared against me.

Beyond the mark of thought; and the high gods,
To do you justice, make them ministers
Of us and those that love you. Best of comfort,
And ever welcome to us!
Agr. Welcome, lady.
Mæc. Welcome, dear madam.
Each heart in Rome does love and pity you.
Only the adulterous Antony, most large
In his abominations, turns you off
And gives his potent regiment to a trull
That noises it against us.
Octa. Is it so, sir?
Cæs. Most certain. Sister, welcome. Pray you
Be ever known to patience. My dear'st sister!
Exeunt.

[Scene VII. Near Actium. Antony's camp.]

Enter Cleopatra and Enobarbus.

Cleo. I will be even with thee, doubt it not.
Eno. But why, why, why?
Cleo. Thou hast forspoke my being in these wars,
And sayst it is not fit.
Eno. Well, is it, is it?
Cleo. If not, denounced against us, why should not we
Be there in person?
Eno. [*Aside*] Well, I could reply:
If we should serve with horse and mares together,

11. **were:** would be; **merely:** completely; **lost:** i.e., useless.

14. **puzzle:** bewilder.

21. **charge:** responsibility.

28. **Tarentum:** a city on the southwest coast of Calabria in southeastern Italy; **Brundusium:** Brindisi, opposite Tarentum on the northeast coast of Calabria.

29. **Ionian sea:** that part of the Mediterranean south of the Adriatic Sea, between Sicily and Greece.

30. **Toryne:** a small town near Actium.

The horse were merely lost; the mares would bear
A soldier and his horse.

Cleo. What is't you say?

Eno. Your presence needs must puzzle Antony;
Take from his heart, take from his brain, from's time,
What should not then be spared. He is already
Traduced for levity, and 'tis said in Rome
That Photinus an eunuch and your maids
Manage this war.

Cleo. Sink Rome, and their tongues rot
That speak against us! A charge we bear i' the war
And, as the president of my kingdom, will
Appear there for a man. Speak not against it.
I will not stay behind!

Enter Antony and Canidius.

Eno. Nay, I have done.
Here comes the Emperor.

Ant. Is it not strange, Canidius,
That from Tarentum and Brundusium
He could so quickly cut the Ionian sea
And take in Toryne?—You have heard on't, sweet?

Cleo. Celerity is never more admired
Than by the negligent.

Ant. A good rebuke,
Which might have well becomed the best of men
To taunt at slackness. Canidius, we
Will fight with him by sea.

Cleo. By sea? What else?

39. **For that:** because.

41. **Pharsalia:** a region in Thessaly, southwestern Greece.

46. **muleteers:** mule drivers.

47. **Engrossed:** amassed; **impress:** conscription.

49. **yare:** manageable, easily maneuvered; see **yarely** [II. ii.] 259.

50. **fall:** befall.

54. **absolute:** perfect; see I. [ii.] 2.

55. **Distract:** divide.

64. **head:** headland.

Can. Why will my lord do so?
Ant. For that he dares us to't.
Eno. So hath my lord dared him to single fight.
Can. Ay, and to wage this battle at Pharsalia,
Where Cæsar fought with Pompey. But these offers,
Which serve not for his vantage, he shakes off;
And so should you.
Eno. Your ships are not well manned;
Your mariners are muleteers, reapers, people
Engrossed by swift impress. In Cæsar's fleet
Are those that often have 'gainst Pompey fought;
Their ships are yare; yours, heavy. No disgrace
Shall fall you for refusing him at sea,
Being prepared for land.
Ant. By sea, by sea!
Eno. Most worthy sir, you therein throw away
The absolute soldiership you have by land;
Distract your army, which doth most consist
Of war-marked footmen; leave unexecuted
Your own renowned knowledge; quite forgo
The way which promises assurance, and
Give up yourself merely to chance and hazard
From firm security.
Ant. I'll fight at sea.
Cleo. I have sixty sails, Cæsar none better.
Ant. Our overplus of shipping will we burn,
And with the rest full-manned, from the head of Actium
Beat the approaching Cæsar. But if we fail,
We then can do't at land.

72. **power:** forces.

75. **Thetis:** one of the Nereids and the mother of Achilles.

85-6. **his whole action grows/Not in the power on't:** his whole campaign is developing without respect to the best use of his military strength.

Roman soldiers—Guillaume Du Choul, *Discours de la religion des anciens Romains* (1556)

Enter a Messenger.

Thy business?
Mess. The news is true, my lord. He is descried;
Cæsar has taken Toryne.
Ant. Can he be there in person? 'Tis impossible;
Strange that his power should be! Canidius,
Our nineteen legions thou shalt hold by land
And our twelve thousand horse. We'll to our ship.
Away, my Thetis!

Enter a Soldier.

How now, worthy soldier?
Sold. O noble Emperor, do not fight by sea!
Trust not to rotten planks. Do you misdoubt
This sword and these my wounds? Let the Egyptians
And the Phoenicians go a-ducking. We
Have used to conquer standing on the earth
And fighting foot to foot.
Ant. Well, well. Away!
Exeunt Antony, Cleopatra, and Enobarbus.
Sold. By Hercules, I think I am i' the right.
Can. Soldier, thou art; but his whole action grows
Not in the power on't. So our leader's led,
And we are women's men.
Sold. You keep by land
The legions and the horse whole, do you not?
Can. Marcus Octavius, Marcus Justeius,
Publicola, and Cælius are for sea;

93. **Carries:** extends.
95. **distractions:** scattered units.
101-2. **throes forth:** painfully produces.

[III. viii.] 6. **prescript:** direction, instruction.
7. **jump:** uncertain venture.

But we keep whole by land. This speed of Cæsar's
Carries beyond belief.
Sold. While he was yet in Rome,
His power went out in such distractions as
Beguiled all spies.
Can. Who's his lieutenant, hear you?
Sold. They say, one Taurus.
Can. Well I know the man.

Enter a Messenger.

Mess. The Emperor calls Canidius.
Can. With news the time's with labor and throes forth
Each minute some.

Exeunt.

[Scene VIII. Actium. A plain.]

Enter Cæsar, with his Army, marching.

Cæs. Taurus!
Taur. My lord?
Cæs. Strike not by land; keep whole: provoke not battle
Till we have done at sea. Do not exceed
The prescript of this scroll. Our fortune lies
Upon this jump.

Exeunt.

[**III. ix.**] 2. **battle:** forces drawn up for battle.

[**III. x.**] 3. **admiral:** flagship, leader of the fleet.
7. **synod:** assembly.
8. **passion:** i.e., specific source of distress.

[Scene IX. The same.]

Enter Antony and Enobarbus.

Ant. Set we our squadrons on yond side o' the hill
In eye of Cæsar's battle; from which place
We may the number of the ships behold,
And so proceed accordingly.

Exeunt.

[Scene X. The same.]

Canidius marcheth with his land army one way over the stage, and Taurus, the Lieutenant of Cæsar, the other way. After their going in is heard the noise of a sea fight.

Alarum. Enter Enobarbus.

Eno. Naught, naught, all naught! I can behold no longer.
The Antoniad, the Egyptian admiral,
With all their sixty, fly and turn the rudder.
To see't mine eyes are blasted.

Enter Scarus.

Scar. Gods and goddesses,
All the whole synod of them!
Eno. What's thy passion?

9. **cantle:** portion.

10. **very:** downright.

13. **tokened pestilence:** the plague, when its presence has been indicated by characteristic spots.

14. **ribald-rid:** an emendation of Nicholas Rowe of the Folio reading "ribaudred," which some editors prefer.

16. **When vantage like a pair of twins appeared:** i.e., when our chances seemed identical with those of the enemy.

18. **breeze:** gadfly.

23. **being luffed:** having turned her vessel's head into the wind and sailed away.

26. **in heighth:** i.e., at its height.

33. **Been what he knew himself:** conducted himself in accordance with his personal bravery and experience in battle.

36. **thereabouts:** that is, of a mind to take flight yourself.

Scar. The greater cantle of the world is lost
With very ignorance. We have kissed away
Kingdoms and provinces.
Eno. How appears the fight?
Scar. On our side like the tokened pestilence
Where death is sure. Yon ribald-rid nag of Egypt
(Whom leprosy o'ertake!) i' the midst o' the fight,
When vantage like a pair of twins appeared,
Both as the same, or rather ours the elder—
The breeze upon her, like a cow in June—
Hoists sails, and flies.
Eno. That I beheld.
Mine eyes did sicken at the sight and could not
Endure a further view.
Scar. She once being luffed,
The noble ruin of her magic, Antony,
Claps on his sea-wing, and (like a doting mallard)
Leaving the fight in heighth, flies after her.
I never saw an action of such shame.
Experience, manhood, honor, ne'er before
Did violate so itself.
Eno. Alack, alack!

Enter Canidius.

Can. Our fortune on the sea is out of breath
And sinks most lamentably. Had our general
Been what he knew himself, it had gone well.
O, he has given example for our flight
Most grossly by his own!
Eno. Ay, are you thereabouts?

38. **Peloponnesus:** the southern part of Greece, connected with central Greece by the Isthmus of Corinth.

39. **attend:** await.

41. **render:** surrender.

45. **wounded chance:** damaged fortune.

46. **Sits in the wind against me:** i.e., strongly opposes me.

[III. xi.] 3. **lated:** i.e., belated (spoken figuratively, as though he were a traveler who had failed to find lodgings for the night before the daylight faded).

Why then, good night indeed.
Can. Toward Peloponnesus are they fled.
Scar. 'Tis easy to't; and there I will attend
What further comes.
Can. To Cæsar will I render
My legions and my horse. Six kings already
Show me the way of yielding.
Eno. I'll yet follow
The wounded chance of Antony, though my reason
Sits in the wind against me.

[*Exeunt.*]

[Scene XI. Alexandria. Cleopatra's Palace.]

Enter Antony with Attendants.

Ant. Hark! the land bids me tread no more upon't!
It is ashamed to bear me! Friends, come hither.
I am so lated in the world that I
Have lost my way forever. I have a ship
Laden with gold. Take that; divide it. Fly,
And make your peace with Cæsar.
Omnes. Fly? Not we!
Ant. I have fled myself, and have instructed cowards
To run and show their shoulders. Friends, be gone.
I have myself resolved upon a course
Which has no need of you. Be gone.

14. **that:** that which, Cleopatra.

15-7. **the white/Reprove the brown for rashness, and they them/For fear and doting:** that is, maturity rebukes his flight for rashness, while youthful spirit blames him for cowardly dotage.

20. **loathness:** reluctance; **hint:** opportunity, as at [III. iv.] 9.

21-2. **Let that be left/Which leaves itself:** i.e., abandon Antony, who has already departed from his true self. Capell corrected the Folio's "Let them" to **Let that; straightway:** directly.

25. **command:** control of his emotions.

My treasure's in the harbor. Take it! O,
I followed that I blush to look upon.
My very hairs do mutiny; for the white
Reprove the brown for rashness, and they them
For fear and doting. Friends, be gone. You shall
Have letters from me to some friends that will
Sweep your way for you. Pray you look not sad
Nor make replies of loathness. Take the hint
Which my despair proclaims. Let that be left
Which leaves itself. To the seaside straightway!
I will possess you of that ship and treasure.
Leave me, I pray, a little; pray you now!
Nay, do so; for indeed I have lost command;
Therefore I pray you. I'll see you by and by.
Sits down.

Enter Cleopatra led by Charmian and Eros,
[Iras following].

Eros. Nay, gentle madam, to him! comfort him!
Iras. Do, most dear Queen.
Char. Do! Why, what else?
Cleo. Let me sit down. O Juno!
Ant. No, no, no, no, no!
Eros. See you here, sir?
Ant. O fie, fie, fie!
Char. Madam!
Iras. Madam, O good Empress!
Eros. Sir, sir!
Ant. Yes, my lord, yes! He at Philippi kept

37-8. **kept/His sword e'en like a dancer:** kept his sword sheathed, as though he were at a ball. Gentlemen wore swords in public at all times, but those for social occasions were usually smaller and lighter.

40. **the mad Brutus ended:** Antony was responsible for the defeat of Brutus, who actually took his own life.

41. **Dealt on lieutenantry:** made war by means of his lieutenants.

42. **brave:** splendid, as used at I. [v.] 44; **squares:** squadrons (drawn up in square formation). In other words, Cæsar himself, according to Antony, never met the enemy face to face.

46. **unqualitied:** unmanned, bereft of the characteristics that determine his quality.

55-6. **I convey my shame out of thine eyes/By looking back what I have left behind:** the meaning is obscure, but it may be something like this: When I look into your eyes, shame is conveyed to me, because I remember the honored career that I have abandoned for you.

57. **Stroyed:** destroyed.

59. **fearful:** full of fear, cowardly.

His sword e'en like a dancer, while I struck
The lean and wrinkled Cassius; and 'twas I
That the mad Brutus ended. He alone
Dealt on lieutenantry and no practice had
In the brave squares of war. Yet now—No matter.

Cleo. Ah, stand by!

Eros. The Queen, my lord, the Queen!

Iras. Go to him, madam, speak to him.
He is unqualitied with very shame.

Cleo. Well then, sustain me. O!

Eros. Most noble sir, arise. The Queen approaches.
Her head's declined, and death will seize her, but
Your comfort makes the rescue.

Ant. I have offended reputation—
A most unnoble swerving.

Eros. Sir, the Queen.

Ant. O, whither hast thou led me, Egypt? See
How I convey my shame out of thine eyes
By looking back what I have left behind
Stroyed in dishonor.

Cleo. O my lord, my lord,
Forgive my fearful sails! I little thought
You would have followed.

Ant. Egypt, thou knewst too well
My heart was to thy rudder tied by the strings,
And thou shouldst tow me after. O'er my spirit
Thy full supremacy thou knewst, and that
Thy beck might from the bidding of the gods
Command me.

Cleo. O, my pardon!

69. **treaties:** entreaties.

70. **palter in the shifts of lowness:** haggle, with the evasions characteristic of the weak.

77. **rates:** is worth.

79. **our schoolmaster:** North's Plutarch indicates that, lacking other trustworthy men to send, they sent their children's tutor, Euphronius, to Cæsar with messages.

Ant. Now I must
To the young man send humble treaties, dodge
And palter in the shifts of lowness, who
With half the bulk o' the world played as I pleased,
Making and marring fortunes. You did know
How much you were my conqueror, and that
My sword, made weak by my affection, would
Obey it on all cause.
Cleo. Pardon, pardon!
Ant. Fall not a tear, I say. One of them rates
All that is won and lost. Give me a kiss.
Even this repays me. We sent our schoolmaster.
Is 'a come back? Love, I am full of lead.
Some wine, within there, and our viands! Fortune knows
We scorn her most when most she offers blows.
Exeunt.

[Scene XII. Egypt. Cæsar's camp.]

Enter Cæsar, Agrippa, Dolabella, [Thidias], with others.

Cæs. Let him appear that's come from Antony.
Know you him?
Dol. Cæsar, 'tis his schoolmaster.
An argument that he is plucked, when hither
He sends so poor a pinion of his wing,
Which had superfluous kings for messengers
Not many moons gone by.

[III. xii.] 10-2. **as petty to his ends/As is the morn-dew on the myrtle leaf/To his grand sea:** the ambassador describes himself as insignificant, like a dewdrop in comparison with the **grand sea** that is Antony.

13. **office:** mission.

15. **Requires:** requests.

21. **circle:** crown, specifically, the traditional crown of the Egyptian monarchy.

22. **hazarded to thy grace:** i.e., a stake which it is in your power to grant to the owner. **Grace** means favor or mercy.

30. **Bring:** escort; **bands:** troops.

Vestal Virgins—Vincenzo Cartari, *Imagini de gli dei de gli antichi* (1609)

Enter [Euphronius,] Ambassador from Antony.

Cæs. Approach and speak.
Amb. Such as I am, I come from Antony.
I was of late as petty to his ends
As is the morn-dew on the myrtle leaf
To his grand sea.
Cæs. Be't so. Declare thine office.
Amb. Lord of his fortunes he salutes thee, and
Requires to live in Egypt; which not granted,
He lessens his requests and to thee sues
To let him breathe between the heavens and earth,
A private man in Athens. This for him.
Next, Cleopatra does confess thy greatness,
Submits her to thy might, and of thee craves
The circle of the Ptolemies for her heirs,
Now hazarded to thy grace.
Cæs. For Antony,
I have no ears to his request. The Queen
Of audience nor desire shall fail, so she
From Egypt drive her all-disgraced friend
Or take his life there. This if she perform,
She shall not sue unheard. So to them both.
Amb. Fortune pursue thee!
Cæs. Bring him through the bands.
[*Exit Ambassador.*]
[*To Thidias*] To try thy eloquence now 'tis time. Dispatch.
From Antony win Cleopatra. Promise,
And in our name, what she requires; add more,

36. **perjure:** cause to commit perjury (breaking of an oath).

37. **Vestal:** priestess of the goddess Vestal or Hestia, who took a vow of perpetual chastity.

41. **becomes his flaw:** adapts himself to his broken fortunes.

42-3. **his very action speaks/In every power that moves:** i.e., Thidias is to observe Antony closely and interpret for Cæsar even the slightest physical gesture that may give a clue to his state of mind.

[III. xiii.] 4. **will:** lust.

6. **ranges:** lines of arrayed ships.

9. **nicked:** marred.

11. **meered question:** limited subject; i.e., the sole cause of hostilities. If the Folio reading is not corrupt, **meered** must derive from "meer" meaning a boundary, but perhaps the word should be corrected to "mere."

12. **course:** chase.

From thine invention, offers. Women are not
In their best fortunes strong, but want will perjure
The ne'er-touched Vestal. Try thy cunning, Thidias.
Make thine own edict for thy pains, which we
Will answer as a law.

Thid. Cæsar, I go.

Cæs. Observe how Antony becomes his flaw,
And what thou thinkst his very action speaks
In every power that moves.

Thid. Cæsar, I shall.

Exeunt.

[Scene XIII. Alexandria. Cleopatra's Palace.]

Enter Cleopatra, Enobarbus, Charmian, and Iras.

Cleo. What shall we do, Enobarbus?

Eno. Think, and die.

Cleo. Is Antony or we in fault for this?

Eno. Antony only, that would make his will
Lord of his reason. What though you fled
From that great face of war whose several ranges
Frighted each other? Why should he follow?
The itch of his affection should not then
Have nicked his captainship, at such a point,
When half to half the world opposed, he being
The meered question. 'Twas a shame no less
Than was his loss, to course your flying flags
And leave his navy gazing.

Cleo. Prithee peace!

21. **grizzled:** flecked with white hairs.

27. **particular:** singular, in the sense "outstanding."

31. **gay:** splendid; **comparisons:** i.e., trappings which surpass Antony's own. Shakespeare probably intended a combination of the meanings of **comparisons** and "caparisons."

32. **answer me declined:** meet my challenge as though he were in reduced circumstances like myself; i.e., horseless, armed only with his sword.

34. **high-battled:** equipped with great armies.

36-7. **Unstate his happiness:** cast aside his good fortune; **staged to the show/Against a sworder:** made into a spectacle (like a public entertainer) by combating a swordsman. Fencing was one of the popular public entertainments of Elizabethan England.

38. **A parcel of:** i.e., consistent with.

Enter the Ambassador [Euphronius] with Antony.

Ant. Is that his answer?
Amb. Ay, my lord.
Ant. The Queen shall then have courtesy, so she
Will yield us up.
Amb. He says so.
Ant. Let her know't.
To the boy Cæsar send this grizzled head,
And he will fill thy wishes to the brim
With principalities.
Cleo. That head, my lord?
Ant. To him again! Tell him he wears the rose
Of youth upon him; from which the world should note
Something particular. His coin, ships, legions
May be a coward's, whose ministers would prevail
Under the service of a child as soon
As i' the command of Cæsar. I dare him therefore
To lay his gay comparisons apart
And answer me declined, sword against sword,
Ourselves alone. I'll write it. Follow me.
[*Exeunt Antony and Ambassador.*]
Eno. [*Aside*] Yes, like enough high-battled Cæsar will
Unstate his happiness and be staged to the show
Against a sworder! I see men's judgments are
A parcel of their fortunes, and things outward
Do draw the inward quality after them
To suffer all alike. That he should dream,

41. **Knowing all measures:** being aware of all the values involved.

42. **Answer:** meet on the same terms, as at l. 32.

46. **blown:** i.e., past its first full flowering, decaying.

48. **honesty:** honor; **square:** quarrel, as at [II.-i.] 55.

55. **apart:** privately.

57. **haply:** perhaps.

59. **Or needs not us:** or he will not have our friendship long. Enobarbus is speaking enigmatically, but his words imply that unless Antony has as many friends as Cæsar his present friends will soon desert him.

Knowing all measures, the full Cæsar will
Answer his emptiness! Cæsar, thou hast subdued
His judgment too.

Enter a Servant.

Serv. A messenger from Cæsar.
Cleo. What, no more ceremony? See, my women!
Against the blown rose may they stop their nose
That kneeled unto the buds. Admit him, sir.
[*Exit Servant.*]
Eno. [*Aside*] Mine honesty and I begin to square.
The loyalty well held to fools does make
Our faith mere folly. Yet he that can endure
To follow with allegiance a fall'n lord
Does conquer him that did his master conquer
And earns a place i' the story.

Enter Thidias.

Cleo. Cæsar's will?
Thid. Hear it apart.
Cleo. None but friends. Say boldly.
Thid. So haply are they friends to Antony.
Eno. He needs as many, sir, as Cæsar has,
Or needs not us. If Cæsar please, our master
Will leap to be his friend. For us, you know
Whose he is we are, and that is Cæsar's.
Thid. So.
Thus then, thou most renowned: Cæsar entreats

64-5. **Not to consider in what case thou standst /Further than he is Cæsar:** i.e., remember that her conqueror is Cæsar (with the implication that mercy is therefore certain).

71. **constrained blemishes:** disgraces forced upon her.

86. **shroud:** protection.

87. **universal landlord:** world's master.

91. **deputation:** Theobald's reading for the Folio "disputation."

Not to consider in what case thou standst
Further than he is Cæsar.

Cleo. Go on. Right royal!

Thid. He knows that you embrace not Antony
As you did love, but as you feared him.

Cleo. O!

Thid. The scars upon your honor, therefore, he
Does pity, as constrained blemishes,
Not as deserved.

Cleo. He is a god, and knows
What is most right. Mine honor was not yielded,
But conquered merely.

Eno. [*Aside*] To be sure of that,
I will ask Antony. Sir, sir, thou art so leaky
That we must leave thee to thy sinking, for
Thy dearest quit thee. *Exit.*

Thid. Shall I say to Cæsar
What you require of him? For he partly begs
To be desired to give. It much would please him
That of his fortunes you should make a staff
To lean upon. But it would warm his spirits
To hear from me you had left Antony
And put yourself under his shroud,
The universal landlord.

Cleo. What's your name?

Thid. My name is Thidias.

Cleo. Most kind messenger,
Say to great Cæsar this: in deputation
I kiss his conqu'ring hand. Tell him I am prompt
To lay my crown at's feet, and there to kneel.

94. **all-obeying breath:** voice which all must obey.

95. **doom:** fate.

97-9. **Wisdom and fortune combating together,/If that the former dare but what it can,/No chance may shake it:** when wisdom combats destiny, it needs only to exert its full power to achieve security; i.e., the greatest safety lies in discretion.

104. **As:** as if.

111. **kite:** a bird of prey, by extension anyone who preys on others, often applied to wantons. Antony is addressing Cleopatra.

114. **muss:** game in which objects were thrown to be scrambled for.

117. **Jack:** low rascal.

118-19. **'Tis better playing with a lion's whelp /Than with an old one dying:** Enobarbus may mean to suggest that the power of Cæsar is less dangerous than Antony's desperation.

Tell him, from his all-obeying breath I hear
The doom of Egypt.

Thid. 'Tis your noblest course.
Wisdom and fortune combating together,
If that the former dare but what it can,
No chance may shake it. Give me grace to lay
My duty on your hand.

Cleo. Your Cæsar's father oft,
When he hath mused of taking kingdoms in,
Bestowed his lips on that unworthy place
As it rained kisses.

Enter Antony and Enobarbus.

Ant. Favors, by Jove that thunders!
What art thou, fellow?

Thid. One that but performs
The bidding of the fullest man, and worthiest
To have command obeyed.

Eno. [*Aside*] You will be whipped.

Ant. Approach there!—Ah, you kite!—Now, gods and devils!
Authority melts from me. Of late, when I cried "Ho!"
Like boys unto a muss, kings would start forth
And cry "Your will?" Have you no ears? I am
Antony yet.

Enter Servants.

Take hence this Jack and whip him.

Eno. [*Aside*] 'Tis better playing with a lion's whelp
Than with an old one dying.

124. **Since she was Cleopatra:** that is, now that she no longer acts like Cleopatra.

125. **cringe his face:** grimace.

131. **blasted:** blighted.

134. **abused:** deceived.

135. **looks on feeders:** shows favor to menials.

137. **boggler:** dissembler; one who moves this way and that as personal advantage dictates.

139. **seel:** sew up. The eyelids of falcons were seeled during the training process to accustom them to wearing a hood. The word is not related to "seal" but derives from the French for eyelash (*cil*).

142. **confusion:** destruction.

147. **Unregist'red in vulgar fame:** unknown in common report.

148. **Luxuriously:** lustfully.

Ant. Moon and stars!
Whip him. Were't twenty of the greatest tributaries
That do acknowledge Cæsar, should I find them
So saucy with the hand of she here—what's her name
Since she was Cleopatra? Whip him, fellows,
Till like a boy you see him cringe his face
And whine aloud for mercy. Take him hence.

Thid. Mark Antony—

Ant. Tug him away. Being whipped,
Bring him again. This Jack of Cæsar's shall
Bear us an errand to him.

Exeunt [Servants] with Thidias.

You were half blasted ere I knew you. Ha!
Have I my pillow left unpressed in Rome,
Forborne the getting of a lawful race,
And by a gem of women, to be abused
By one that looks on feeders?

Cleo. Good my lord—

Ant. You have been a boggler ever.
But when we in our viciousness grow hard
(O misery on't!) the wise gods seel our eyes,
In our own filth drop our clear judgments, make us
Adore our errors, laugh at's while we strut
To our confusion.

Cleo. O, is't come to this?

Ant. I found you as a morsel cold upon
Dead Cæsar's trencher. Nay, you were a fragment
Of Gnæus Pompey's, besides what hotter hours,
Unregist'red in vulgar fame, you have
Luxuriously picked out: for I am sure,

153. **quit:** requite, reward.

155. **high:** noble.

156. **the hill of Bashan:** a reference to the biblical bulls of Bashan, see Psalms 68:15 and 22:12-3. Antony feels that no one has ever been so notoriously cuckolded.

160. **yare:** deft, quick; see [II. ii.] 259 and [III. vii.] 49.

163. **'a:** he.

172. **entertainment:** reception.

Though you can guess what temperance should be,
You know not what it is.
Cleo. Wherefore is this?
Ant. To let a fellow that will take rewards,
And say "God quit you!" be familiar with
My playfellow, your hand, this kingly seal
And plighter of high hearts! O that I were
Upon the hill of Bashan to outroar
The horned herd! for I have savage cause,
And to proclaim it civilly were like
A haltered neck which does the hangman thank
For being yare about him.

Enter a Servant with Thidias.

Is he whipped?
Serv. Soundly, my lord.
Ant. Cried he? and begged 'a pardon?
Serv. He did ask favor.
Ant. If that thy father live, let him repent
Thou wast not made his daughter; and be thou sorry
To follow Cæsar in his triumph, since
Thou hast been whipped for following him. Henceforth
The white hand of a lady fever thee!
Shake thou to look on't! Get thee back to Cæsar;
Tell him thy entertainment. Look thou say
He makes me angry with him; for he seems
Proud and disdainful, harping on what I am,
Not what he knew I was. He makes me angry;
And at this time most easy 'tis to do't,

178. **orbs:** spheres.

181. **enfranched:** freed.

183. **quit me:** pay me back; **Urge:** mention.

186. **our terrene moon:** Cleopatra, who is the earthly personification of Isis, the moon goddess.

189. **stay his time:** wait until he is ready to listen to me.

191. **points:** laces, the fastenings of his garments.

197. **determines:** terminates, melts.

198. **smite:** Rowe's correction of the Folio reading "smile."

201. **discandying:** melting. Theobald suggested this for the Folio "discandering."

206. **fate:** victorious destiny.

Isis—Guillaume Rouillé, *Promptuarii iconum* (1553) (See 1. v. 55.)

When my good stars that were my former guides
Have empty left their orbs and shot their fires
Into the abysm of hell. If he mislike
My speech and what is done, tell him he has
Hipparchus, my enfranched bondman, whom
He may at pleasure whip or hang or torture,
As he shall like, to quit me. Urge it thou.
Hence with thy stripes, be gone!

Exit Thidias.

Cleo. Have you done yet?
Ant. Alack, our terrene moon
Is now eclipsed, and it portends alone
The fall of Antony!
Cleo. I must stay his time.
Ant. To flatter Cæsar, would you mingle eyes
With one that ties his points?
Cleo. Not know me yet?
Ant. Cold-hearted toward me?
Cleo. Ah, dear, if I be so,
From my cold heart let heaven engender hail,
And poison it in the source, and the first stone
Drop in my neck; as it determines, so
Dissolve my life! The next Cæsarion smite!
Till by degrees the memory of my womb,
Together with my brave Egyptians all,
By the discandying of this pelleted storm,
Lie graveless, till the flies and gnats of Nile
Have buried them for prey!
Ant. I am satisfied.
Cæsar sits down in Alexandria, where
I will oppose his fate. Our force by land

207-8. **our severed navy . . ./Have knit again, and fleet:** our scattered ships are reassembled and float again.

217. **maliciously:** violently.

218. **nice:** finicky, governed only by my whims of taste.

221. **gaudy:** festive.

Hath nobly held; our severed navy too
Have knit again, and fleet, threat'ning most sea-like.
Where hast thou been, my heart? Dost thou hear, lady?
If from the field I shall return once more
To kiss these lips, I will appear in blood.
I and my sword will earn our chronicle.
There's hope in't yet.

Cleo. That's my brave lord!

Ant. I will be treble-sinewed, hearted, breathed,
And fight maliciously. For when mine hours
Were nice and lucky, men did ransom lives
Of me for jests; but now I'll set my teeth
And send to darkness all that stop me. Come,
Let's have one other gaudy night. Call to me
All my sad captains; fill our bowls once more.
Let's mock the midnight bell.

Cleo. It is my birthday.
I had thought t' have held it poor; but since my lord
Is Antony again, I will be Cleopatra.

Ant. We will yet do well.

Cleo. Call all his noble captains to my lord.

Ant. Do so, we'll speak to them; and tonight I'll force
The wine peep through their scars. Come on, my queen,
There's sap in't yet! The next time I do fight,
I'll make Death love me; for I will contend
Even with his pestilent scythe.

Exeunt [all but Enobarbus].

238. **estridge:** ostrich. The word may also refer to a goshawk or falcon.

240-41. **When valor preys on reason,/It eats the sword it fights with:** i.e., "Discretion is the better part of valor."

Eno. Now he'll outstare the lightning. To be furious
Is to be frighted out of fear, and in that mood
The dove will peck the estridge. I see still
A diminution in our captain's brain
Restores his heart. When valor preys on reason,
It eats the sword it fights with. I will seek
Some way to leave him.

Exit.

ANTONY AND CLEOPATRA

ACT IV

[IV.] Antony prepares to meet Cæsar's forces, which contain many of his own deserters. Learning that Enobarbus has deserted, he sends after him his abandoned treasure. Antony blames himself for Enobarbus' faithlessness. The latter dies of a broken heart on receiving this token of Antony's generosity.

Victorious in the first engagement, Antony later meets disaster when his fleet deserts to the enemy. Desperate with rage and shame, Antony charges Cleopatra with treachery. She takes refuge in her burial monument and, to allay his anger, sends word that she is dead. Antony in grief gives himself a mortal wound. Cleopatra has the wounded Antony drawn up to die beside her. Though she grieves, his death exalts her, and Cleopatra contemplates her own suicide, "after the high Roman fashion."

[IV. i.] 1. **as:** as if.

10. **breath:** breathing space, time to recover himself.

11. **boot:** profit.

15. **files:** ranks of men, as at I. i. 3.

17. **fetch him in:** capture him.

[*ACT IV*]

[Scene I. Alexandria. Cæsar's camp.]

Enter Cæsar, Agrippa, and Mæcenas, with his Army; Cæsar reading a letter.

Cæs. He calls me boy, and chides as he had power
To beat me out of Egypt. My messenger
He hath whipped with rods; dares me to personal
combat,
Cæsar to Antony. Let the old ruffian know
I have many other ways to die, meantime
Laugh at his challenge.
Mæc. Cæsar must think,
When one so great begins to rage, he's hunted
Even to falling. Give him no breath, but now
Make boot of his distraction. Never anger
Made good guard for itself.
Cæs. Let our best heads
Know that tomorrow the last of many battles
We mean to fight. Within our files there are,
Of those that served Mark Antony but late,
Enough to fetch him in. See it done;
And feast the army. We have store to do't,
And they have earned the waste. Poor Antony!
Exeunt.

[IV. ii.] 8, 9. **Or . . ./Or:** either . . . or.
10. **Woo't:** wilt, will you.
11. **Take all:** i.e., "Winner take all."
16. **honest:** faithful.

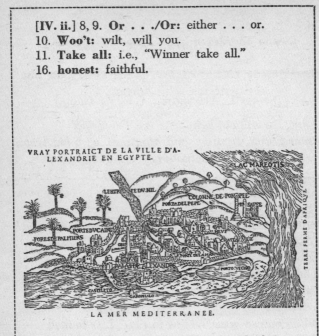

Ancient Alexandria—Pierre Belon, *Observations de plusieurs singularitez* (1588)

[Scene II. Alexandria. Cleopatra's Palace.]

Enter Antony, Cleopatra, Enobarbus, Charmian, Iras, Alexas, with others.

Ant. He will not fight with me, Domitius?
Eno. No.
Ant. Why should he not?
Eno. He thinks, being twenty times of better fortune,
He is twenty men to one.
Ant. Tomorrow, soldier,
By sea and land I'll fight. Or I will live,
Or bathe my dying honor in the blood
Shall make it live again. Woo't thou fight well?
Eno. I'll strike, and cry "Take all!"
Ant. Well said. Come on.
Call forth my household servants. Let's tonight
Be bounteous at our meal.

Enter three or four Servitors.

Give me thy hand,
Thou hast been rightly honest. So hast thou;
And thou, and thou, and thou. You have served me well,
And kings have been your fellows.
Cleo. [*Aside to Enobarbus*] What means this?
Eno. [*Aside to Cleopatra*] 'Tis one of those odd tricks which sorrow shoots
Out of the mind.

38. **period:** end.
46. **yield:** reward.

Ant. And thou art honest too.
I wish I could be made so many men,
And all of you clapped up together in
An Antony, that I might do you service
So good as you have done.
Omnes. The gods forbid!
Ant. Well, my good fellows, wait on me tonight.
Scant not my cups, and make as much of me
As when mine empire was your fellow too
And suffered my command.
Cleo. [*Aside to Enobarbus*] What does he mean?
Eno. [*Aside to Cleopatra*] To make his followers
weep.
Ant. Tend me tonight.
Maybe it is the period of your duty.
Haply you shall not see me more; or if,
A mangled shadow. Perchance tomorrow
You'll serve another master. I look on you
As one that takes his leave. Mine honest friends,
I turn you not away; but, like a master
Married to your good service, stay till death.
Tend me tonight two hours, I ask no more,
And the gods yield you for't!
Eno. What mean you, sir,
To give them this discomfort? Look, they weep,
And I, an ass, am onion-eyed. For shame!
Transform us not to women.
Ant. Ho, ho, ho!
Now the witch take me if I meant it thus!
Grace grow where those drops fall! My hearty friends,
You take me in too dolorous a sense;

60. **consideration:** reflection.

[IV. iii.] 5. **Belike:** most likely.

For I spake to you for your comfort, did desire you
To burn this night with torches. Know, my hearts,
I hope well of tomorrow, and will lead you
Where rather I'll expect victorious life
Than death and honor. Let's to supper, come,
And drown consideration.

Exeunt.

[Scene III. Alexandria. Before Cleopatra's Palace.]

Enter a Company of Soldiers.

1. *Sold.* Brother, good night. Tomorrow is the day.
2. *Sold.* It will determine one way. Fare you well.
Heard you of nothing strange about the streets?
1. *Sold.* Nothing. What news?
2. *Sold.* Belike 'tis but a rumor. Good night to you.
1. *Sold.* Well, sir, good night.

They meet other Soldiers.

2. *Sold.* Soldiers, have careful watch.
3. *Sold.* And you. Good night, good night.

They place themselves in every corner of the stage.

2. *Sold.* Here we. And if tomorrow
Our navy thrive, I have an absolute hope
Our landmen will stand up.

S.D. after l. 13. **hautboys:** oboes.

19. **signs:** omens, is a good omen.

32. **so far as we have quarter:** to the limits of our assigned posts.

33. **give off:** finish.

1. Sold. 'Tis a brave army,
And full of purpose.

Music of the hautboys is under the stage.

2. Sold. Peace! What noise?

1. Sold. List, list!

2. Sold. Hark!

1. Sold. Music i' the air.

3. Sold. Under the earth.

4. Sold. It signs well, does it not?

3. Sold. No.

1. Sold. Peace, I say!
What should this mean?

2. Sold. 'Tis the god Hercules, whom Antony loved,
Now leaves him.

1. Sold. Walk. Let's see if other watchmen
Do hear what we do.

2. Sold. How now, masters?

Speak together.

Omnes. How now?
How now? Do you hear this?

1. Sold. Ay. Is't not strange?

3. Sold. Do you hear, masters? Do you hear?

1. Sold. Follow the noise so far as we have quarter.
Let's see how it will give off.

Omnes. Content. 'Tis strange.

Exeunt.

[IV. iv.] 12. **Sooth:** truly.

20. **daff't:** doff it.

22. **tight:** competent.

[Scene IV. Alexandria. Cleopatra's Palace.]

Enter Antony and Cleopatra, [Charmian, Iras,] with others.

Ant. Eros! mine armor, Eros!
Cleo. Sleep a little.
Ant. No, my chuck. Eros! Come, mine armor, Eros!

Enter Eros [with armor].

Come, good fellow, put mine iron on.
If Fortune be not ours today, it is
Because we brave her. Come.
Cleo. Nay, I'll help too.
What's this for?
Ant. Ah, let be, let be! Thou art
The armorer of my heart. False, false! This, this!
Cleo. Sooth, la, I'll help. Thus it must be.
Ant. Well, well,
We shall thrive now. Seest thou, my good fellow?
Go put on thy defenses.
Eros. Briefly, sir.
Cleo. Is not this buckled well?
Ant. Rarely, rarely!
He that unbuckles this, till we do please
To daff't for our repose, shall hear a storm.
Thou fumblest, Eros, and my queen's a squire
More tight at this than thou. Dispatch. O love,
That thou couldst see my wars today, and knewst

25. **workman:** craftsman.

27. **charge:** task.

28. **betime:** early.

31. **riveted trim:** i.e., armored equipment.

32. **port:** portal, gate.

38. **Well said:** well done.

41-2. **check:** rebuke; **stand/On:** insist upon; **mechanic compliment:** vulgar ceremony of leavetaking. Antony probably means that he and Cleopatra are too noble for the tears and pathetic words that would accompany the farewells of common lovers. **Mechanic** is an epithet applied to people who work with their hands; hence, the lower sort.

The royal occupation! Thou shouldst see
A workman in't.

Enter an armed Soldier.

Good morrow to thee! Welcome.
Thou lookst like him that knows a warlike charge.
To business that we love we rise betime
And go to't with delight.
Sold. A thousand, sir,
Early though't be, have on their riveted trim
And at the port expect you.

Shout. Trumpets. Flourish. Enter Captains and Soldiers.

Capt. The morn is fair. Good morrow, General.
All. Good morrow, General.
Ant. 'Tis well blown, lads.
This morning, like the spirit of a youth
That means to be of note, begins betimes.
So, so. Come, give me that! This way. Well said.
Fare thee well, dame, whate'er becomes of me.
This is a soldier's kiss. Rebukable
And worthy shameful check it were to stand
On more mechanic compliment. I'll leave thee
Now like a man of steel. You that will fight,
Follow me close; I'll bring you to't. Adieu.
Exeunt [Antony, Eros, Captains, and Soldiers].
Char. Please you retire to your chamber?

[IV. v.] 2. **Would:** would that.

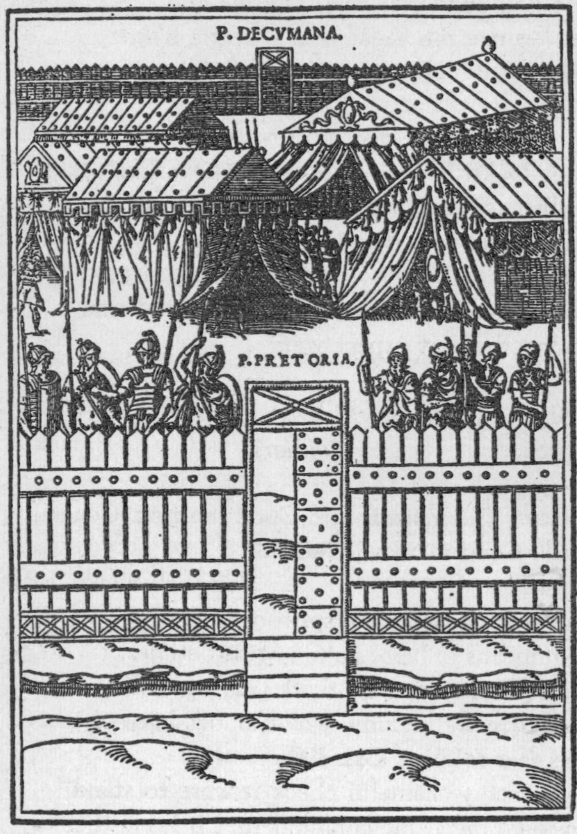

A Roman camp—Guillaume Du Choul, *Discours de la religion des anciens Romains* (1556)

Cleo. Lead me.
He goes forth gallantly. That he and Cæsar might
Determine this great war in single fight!
Then Antony—but now—Well, on!

Exeunt.

[Scene V. Alexandria. Antony's camp.]

Trumpets sound. Enter Antony and Eros,
[*a Soldier meeting them*].

Sold. The gods make this a happy day to Antony!
Ant. Would thou and those thy scars had once prevailed
To make me fight at land!
Sold. Hadst thou done so,
The kings that have revolted and the soldier
That has this morning left thee would have still
Followed thy heels.
Ant. Who's gone this morning?
Sold. Who?
One ever near thee. Call for Enobarbus,
He shall not hear thee, or from Cæsar's camp
Say "I am none of thine."
Ant. What sayest thou?
Sold. Sir,
He is with Cæsar.
Eros. Sir, his chests and treasure
He has not with him.
Ant. Is he gone?

[IV. vi.] 6. **three-nooked:** three-cornered, the corners consisting of Europe, Africa, and Asia.

11. **those that have revolted:** the deserters from Antony's own ranks; **van:** vanguard, forefront.

Sold. Most certain.
Ant. Go, Eros, send his treasure after. Do it;
Detain no jot, I charge thee. Write to him
(I will subscribe) gentle adieus and greetings.
Say that I wish he never find more cause
To change a master. O, my fortunes have
Corrupted honest men! Dispatch. Enobarbus!
Exeunt.

[Scene VI. Alexandria. Cæsar's camp.]

Flourish. Enter Agrippa, Cæsar, with Enobarbus, and Dolabella.

Cæs. Go forth, Agrippa, and begin the fight.
Our will is Antony be took alive.
Make it so known.
Agr. Cæsar, I shall. [*Exit.*]
Cæs. The time of universal peace is near.
Prove this a prosp'rous day, the three-nooked world
Shall bear the olive freely.

Enter a Messenger.

Mess. Antony
Is come into the field.
Cæs. Go charge Agrippa
Plant those that have revolted in the van,
That Antony may seem to spend his fury
Upon himself.
Exeunt [all but Enobarbus].

15. **dissuade:** persuade.
19. **entertainment:** employment.
30. **safed:** provided safe conduct for.
37. **turpitude:** vile behavior.
38. **blows:** swells.
39. **thought:** sorrow.

Eno. Alexas did revolt and went to Jewry on
Affairs of Antony; there did dissuade
Great Herod to incline himself to Cæsar
And leave his master Antony. For this pains
Cæsar hath hanged him. Canidius and the rest
That fell away have entertainment, but
No honorable trust. I have done ill,
Of which I do accuse myself so sorely
That I will joy no more.

Enter a Soldier of Cæsar's.

Sold. Enobarbus, Antony
Hath after thee sent all thy treasure, with
His bounty overplus. The messenger
Came on my guard and at thy tent is now
Unloading of his mules.

Eno. I give it you!

Sold. Mock not, Enobarbus.
I tell you true. Best you safed the bringer
Out of the host. I must attend mine office
Or would have done't myself. Your emperor
Continues still a Jove. *Exit.*

Eno. I am alone the villain of the earth,
And feel I am so most. O Antony,
Thou mine of bounty, how wouldst thou have paid
My better service, when my turpitude
Thou dost so crown with gold! This blows my heart.
If swift thought break it not, a swifter mean
Shall outstrike thought; but thought will do't, I feel.

[IV. vii.] 2-3. **has work:** is hard pressed; **our oppression/Exceeds what we expected:** the enemy presses us more heavily than we expected.

6. **clouts:** cloths, bandages.

9. **made an H:** a characteristic Elizabethan pun. The word "ache" was pronounced "aitch."

11. **bench holes:** privies.

12. **scotches:** slashes, wounds.

13-4. **our advantage serves/For a fair victory:** the advantage we have now equals a fine victory.

I fight against thee? No! I will go seek
Some ditch wherein to die; the foul'st best fits
My latter part of life.

Exit.

[Scene VII. Field of battle between the camps.]

Alarum. Drum and Trumpets. Enter Agrippa [and others].

Agr. Retire. We have engaged ourselves too far.
Cæsar himself has work, and our oppression
Exceeds what we expected. *Exeunt.*

Alarums. Enter Antony, and Scarus, wounded.

Scar. O my brave Emperor, this is fought indeed!
Had we done so at first, we had droven them home
With clouts about their heads.

Ant. Thou bleedst apace.

Scar. I had a wound here that was like a T,
But now 'tis made an H. [*Retreat sounded*] *far off.*

Ant. They do retire.

Scar. We'll beat 'em into bench holes. I have yet
Room for six scotches more.

Enter Eros.

Eros. They are beaten, sir, and our advantage serves
For a fair victory.

Scar. Let us score their backs
And snatch 'em up, as we take hares, behind!
'Tis sport to maul a runner.

Ant. I will reward thee

19. **sprightly:** cheerful.

21. **halt:** limp.

[IV. viii.] 2. **gests:** exploits.

7. **shown all Hectors:** all appeared Hectors in your valor. Hector was a famous Trojan warrior, son of King Priam of Troy.

8. **clip:** embrace.

13. **fairy:** an appropriate term for Cleopatra because of her power to charm men. Fairies were also supposed to grant good fortune to humans whom they favored.

15. **day o' the world:** i.e., sun that lights the world.

17. **proof of harness:** proof armor; that is, armor designed to be impenetrable.

Once for thy sprightly comfort, and tenfold
For thy good valor. Come thee on!
Scar. I'll halt after.
Exeunt.

[Scene VIII. Under the walls of Alexandria.]

Alarum. Enter Antony again in a march; Scarus, with others.

Ant. We have beat him to his camp. Run one before
And let the Queen know of our gests. Tomorrow,
Before the sun shall see's, we'll spill the blood
That has today escaped. I thank you all;
For doughty-handed are you, and have fought
Not as you served the cause, but as't had been
Each man's like mine. You have shown all Hectors.
Enter the city, clip your wives, your friends,
Tell them your feats, whilst they with joyful tears
Wash the congealment from your wounds and kiss
The honored gashes whole.

Enter Cleopatra [attended].

[*To Scarus*] Give me thy hand.—
To this great fairy I'll commend thy acts,
Make her thanks bless thee. [*To Cleopatra*] O thou day o' the world,
Chain mine armed neck! Leap thou, attire and all,
Through proof of harness to my heart, and there
Ride on the pants triumphing!

20. **virtue:** valor.

25. **something:** somewhat.

29. **Commend:** entrust.

35. **carbuncled:** set with gems. The chariot of Phoebus is so described in Ovid's *Metamorphoses*, Book 2, ll. 107-11.

38. **owe:** own.

44. **taborins:** drums.

Cleo. Lord of lords!
O infinite virtue, comest thou smiling from
The world's great snare uncaught?
Ant. My nightingale,
We have beat them to their beds. What, girl! though grey
Do something mingle with our younger brown, yet ha' we
A brain that nourishes our nerves, and can
Get goal for goal of youth. Behold this man.
Commend unto his lips thy favoring hand.—
Kiss it, my warrior!—He hath fought today
As if a god in hate of mankind had
Destroyed in such a shape.
Cleo. I'll give thee, friend,
An armor all of gold. It was a king's.
Ant. He has deserved it, were it carbuncled
Like holy Phoebus' car. Give me thy hand.
Through Alexandria make a jolly march;
Bear our hacked targets like the men that owe them.
Had our great palace the capacity
To camp this host, we all would sup together
And drink carouses to the next day's fate,
Which promises royal peril. Trumpeters,
With brazen din blast you the city's ear;
Make mingle with our rattling taborins,
That heaven and earth may strike their sounds together,
Applauding our approach.

Exeunt.

[IV. ix.] 2. **court of guard:** guard room.

3. **embattle:** take our battle stations.

6. **shrewd:** cursed, grievous.

9. **close:** concealed or quiet.

17. **melancholy:** melancholia, which was believed to be the result of the moon's influence.

18. **disponge:** squeeze out.

25. **in thine own particular:** personally.

[Scene IX. Cæsar's camp.]

Enter a Sentry and his Company. Enobarbus follows.

Sent. If we be not relieved within this hour,
We must return to the court of guard. The night
Is shiny, and they say we shall embattle
By the second hour i' the morn.
1. Watch. This last day was
A shrewd one to's.
Eno. O, bear me witness, night—
2. Watch. What man is this?
1. Watch. Stand close, and list him.
Eno. Be witness to me, O thou blessed moon,
When men revolted shall upon record
Bear hateful memory, poor Enobarbus did
Before thy face repent!
Sent. Enobarbus?
2. Watch. Peace!
Hark further.
Eno. O sovereign mistress of true melancholy,
The poisonous damp of night disponge upon me,
That life, a very rebel to my will,
May hang no longer on me! Throw my heart
Against the flint and hardness of my fault,
Which, being dried with grief, will break to powder,
And finish all foul thoughts. O Antony,
Nobler than my revolt is infamous,
Forgive me in thine own particular,
But let the world rank me in register

39. **raught:** grasped. This is the past participle of "reach."

41. **Demurely:** gently.

A master-leaver and a fugitive!
O Antony! O Antony! [*Dies.*]

1. Watch. Let's speak
To him.

Sent. Let's hear him, for the things he speaks
May concern Cæsar.

2. Watch. Let's do so. But he sleeps.

Sent. Swoons rather; for so bad a prayer as his
Was never yet for sleep.

1. Watch. Go we to him.

2. Watch. Awake, sir, awake! Speak to us!

1. Watch. Hear you, sir?

Sent. The hand of death hath raught him.

Drums afar off.

Hark! The drums
Demurely wake the sleepers. Let us bear him
To the court of guard. He is of note. Our hour
Is fully out.

2. Watch. Come on then.
He may recover yet.

Exeunt [*with the body*].

[Scene X. Between the two camps.]

Enter Antony and Scarus, with their Army.

Ant. Their preparation is today by sea;
We please them not by land.

Scar. For both, my lord.

[IV. x.] 5. **foot:** foot soldiers.

[IV. xi.] 1. **But being charged, we will be still by land:** unless they charge us, we will be inactive by land.

4. **hold our best advantage:** take up the best position for our advantage.

[IV. xii.] 1. **joined:** engaged in battle.

4. **Straight:** directly.

6. **augurers:** soothsayers, whose duty it was to interpret omens.

Roman augurers—Guillaume Du Choul, *Discours de la religion des anciens Romains* (1556)

Ant. I would they'ld fight i' the fire or i' the air;
We'ld fight there too. But this it is, our foot
Upon the hills adjoining to the city
Shall stay with us. Order for sea is given;
They have put forth the haven,
Where their appointment we may best discover
And look on their endeavor.

Exeunt.

[Scene XI. Between the camps.]

Enter Cæsar and his Army.

Cæs. But being charged, we will be still by land,
Which, as I tak't, we shall; for his best force
Is forth to man his galleys. To the vales,
And hold our best advantage.

Exeunt.

[Scene XII. Alexandria. A hill overlooking the harbor.]

Enter Antony and Scarus.

Ant. Yet they are not joined. Where yond pine does stand
I shall discover all. I'll bring thee word
Straight how 'tis like to go. *Exit.*

Scar. Swallows have built
In Cleopatra's sails their nests. The augurers

10. **fretted:** checkered, composed of both favorable and unfavorable elements.

19. **charm:** charmer.

24. **spanieled:** Hanmer's emendation of the Folio's meaningless "pannelled."

25. **discandy:** melt, as at [III. xiii.] 201.

28. **grave charm:** deadly witch.

Say they know not, they cannot tell; look grimly
And dare not speak their knowledge. Antony
Is valiant, and dejected; and by starts
His fretted fortunes give him hope and fear
Of what he has and has not.

Alarum afar off, as at a sea fight.

Enter Antony.

Ant. All is lost!
This foul Egyptian hath betrayed me!
My fleet hath yielded to the foe, and yonder
They cast their caps up and carouse together
Like friends long lost. Triple-turned whore! 'tis thou
Hast sold me to this novice, and my heart
Makes only wars on thee. Bid them all fly!
For when I am revenged upon my charm,
I have done all. Bid them all fly; begone!

[*Exit Scarus.*]

O sun, thy uprise shall I see no more.
Fortune and Antony part here; even here
Do we shake hands. All come to this? The hearts
That spanieled me at heels, to whom I gave
Their wishes, do discandy, melt their sweets
On blossoming Cæsar; and this pine is barked,
That overtopped them all. Betrayed I am.
O this false soul of Egypt! this grave charm—
Whose eye becked forth my wars and called them home,

32. **right:** veritable; **fast and loose:** a trick employed by mountebanks with a belt or string, the point of which was the tying of a knot which appeared firm but would readily yield to the touch.

33. **Beguiled:** cheated; **the very heart of loss:** absolute ruin.

35. **Avaunt:** begone.

38. **blemish Caesar's triumph:** i.e., deprive Cæsar's triumphal procession of its chief ornament, the living Cleopatra.

40. **spot:** disgrace.

41. **monster-like:** that is, as though she were a freak.

42. **poor'st diminutives:** petty sums of money. A **doit** was a small copper coin.

47-8. **one death/Might have prevented many:** Antony means that she will die many deaths in the shame that awaits her as Cæsar's prize.

49. **The shirt of Nessus:** Nessus was a centaur whom Hercules wounded with a poisoned arrow defending his wife, Dejanira, from the centaur's advances. In revenge, Nessus gave a cloak which had been drenched in his blood to Dejanira and tricked her into giving it to Hercules, who was consumed by mortal agony when he put it on and threw the bearer of the gift, Lichas, into the sea.

50. **Alcides:** another name for Hercules.

Whose bosom was my crownet, my chief end–
Like a right gypsy hath at fast and loose
Beguiled me to the very heart of loss!
What, Eros, Eros!

Enter Cleopatra.

Ah, thou spell! Avaunt!
Cleo. Why is my lord enraged against his love?
Ant. Vanish, or I shall give thee thy deserving
And blemish Cæsar's triumph. Let him take thee
And hoist thee up to the shouting plebeians.
Follow his chariot, like the greatest spot
Of all thy sex. Most monster-like be shown
For poor'st diminutives, for doits, and let
Patient Octavia plough thy visage up
With her prepared nails.

Exit Cleopatra.

'Tis well th'art gone,
If it be well to live; but better 'twere
Thou fellst into my fury, for one death
Might have prevented many. Eros, ho!
The shirt of Nessus is upon me. Teach me,
Alcides, thou mine ancestor, thy rage.
Let me lodge Lichas on the horns o' the moon
And with those hands that grasped the heaviest club
Subdue my worthiest self. The witch shall die.
To the young Roman boy she hath sold me, and I fall
Under this plot. She dies for't. Eros, ho!

Exit.

[IV. xiii.] 2. **Telamon:** Ajax, son of Telamon, who went mad when the shield of Achilles was awarded to Ulysses instead of to himself; **boar of Thessaly:** a ferocious boar loosed on Calydon as Diana's revenge for neglecting her worship.

3. **embossed:** driven to extremity like a hunted animal; hence, savagely angry.

4. **monument:** tomb, which, in accordance with Egyptian custom, Cleopatra had caused to be erected for her burial.

6-7. **The soul and body rive not more in parting/Than greatness going off:** even the rupture between soul and body at death is less violent than the explosive rage of a noble person.

Hercules and Lichas–Ovid, *Metamorphoses* (1565)
(See IV. xii. 50.)

[Scene XIII. Alexandria. Cleopatra's Palace.]

Enter Cleopatra, Charmian, Iras, Mardian.

Cleo. Help me, my women! O, he is more mad
Than Telamon for his shield. The boar of Thessaly
Was never so embossed.
Char. To the monument!
There lock yourself, and send him word you are dead.
The soul and body rive not more in parting
Than greatness going off.
Cleo. To the monument!
Mardian, go tell him I have slain myself.
Say that the last I spoke was "Antony"
And word it, prithee, piteously. Hence, Mardian,
And bring me how he takes my death. To the monument!

Exeunt.

[Scene XIV. Another room in Cleopatra's Palace.]

Enter Antony and Eros.

Ant. Eros, thou yet beholdst me?
Eros. Ay, noble lord.
Ant. Sometime we see a cloud that's dragonish;
A vapor sometime like a bear or lion,
A towered citadel, a pendent rock,
A forked mountain, or blue promontory

[IV. xiv.] 10. **Vesper:** night; **pageants:** illusory spectacles. **Pageants** were regularly part of the festivities when monarchs made formal progresses. By analogy, the cloud shapes Antony describes precede the coming of night.

14. **rack:** cloud drift; **dislimns:** effaces.

23. **mo:** more.

24. **Packed cards:** joined in stacking the deck.

25. **triumph:** a pun. The triumph was the prize or "trump" card in a game of the same name.

29. **robbed me of my sword:** i.e., rendered me defenseless before my enemy.

With trees upon't that nod unto the world
And mock our eyes with air. Thou hast seen these signs;
They are black Vesper's pageants.
Eros. Ay, my lord.
Ant. That which is now a horse, even with a thought
The rack dislimns, and makes it indistinct
As water is in water.
Eros. It does, my lord.
Ant. My good knave Eros, now thy captain is
Even such a body. Here I am Antony;
Yet cannot hold this visible shape, my knave.
I made these wars for Egypt; and the Queen—
Whose heart I thought I had, for she had mine,
Which, whilst it was mine, had annexed unto't
A million mo, now lost—she, Eros, has
Packed cards with Cæsar and false-played my glory
Unto an enemy's triumph.
Nay, weep not, gentle Eros. There is left us
Ourselves to end ourselves.

Enter Mardian.

O, thy vile lady!
She has robbed me of my sword.
Mar. No, Antony.
My mistress loved thee and her fortunes mingled
With thine entirely.
Ant. Hence, saucy eunuch! Peace!
She hath betrayed me and shall die the death.

41. **rend'red:** surrendered.

50. **sevenfold shield of Ajax:** Ajax had a famous shield containing seven folds of oxhide. Ovid has him argue in defense of his claim to Achilles' shield that his own contained many dents as the result of his valorous exploits (*Metamorphoses,* Book 13).

52. **continent:** container.

58. **length:** i.e., of life; **torch:** that is, the lighter of his ways—Cleopatra. He speaks as though he were a night traveler.

60-1. **very force entangles/Itself with strength:** i.e., the violence of his efforts combats the effectiveness of his strength; **Seal:** affix the seal signifying completion, as on a document.

63. **Where souls do couch on flowers:** the Elysian Fields; **hand in hand:** a verb like "move" is understood.

Mar. Death of one person can be paid but once,
And that she has discharged. What thou wouldst do
Is done unto thy hand. The last she spake
Was, "Antony! most noble Antony!"
Then in the midst a tearing groan did break
The name of Antony; it was divided
Between her heart and lips. She rend'red life,
Thy name so buried in her.

Ant. Dead, then?

Mar. Dead.

Ant. Unarm, Eros. The long day's task is done,
And we must sleep. [*To Mardian*] That thou departst hence safe
Does pay thy labor richly. Go. *Exit Mardian.*
Off, pluck off!
The sevenfold shield of Ajax cannot keep
The battery from my heart. O, cleave, my sides!
Heart, once be stronger than thy continent,
Crack thy frail case! Apace, Eros, apace.—
No more a soldier. Bruised pieces, go;
You have been nobly borne.—From me awhile.
Exit Eros.
I will o'ertake thee, Cleopatra, and
Weep for my pardon. So it must be, for now
All length is torture. Since the torch is out,
Lie down, and stray no farther. Now all labor
Mars what it does; yea, very force entangles
Itself with strength. Seal then, and all is done.
Eros!—I come, my queen.—Eros!—Stay for me.
Where souls do couch on flowers, we'll hand in hand

64. **port:** comportment, behavior.

65. **Dido and her Æneas:** Dido, queen of Carthage, and Æneas, founder of Rome, a famous pair of lovers in Virgil's *Æneid;* **want troops:** lack admirers.

66. **haunt:** resort; i.e., everyone will flock to us.

71. **green Neptune:** the ocean, of which Neptune was the god.

76. **exigent:** exigency, crisis.

78. **inevitable prosecution:** inescapable pursuit.

88. **pleached:** i.e., crossed and tied together as a captive.

89-90. **corrigible:** submissive to correction; **subdued/To penetrative shame:** conquered by acute shame.

90-2. **the wheeled seat/Of fortunate Caesar, drawn before him, branded/His baseness that ensued:** i.e., Cæsar's good fortune in riding before him in a triumphal chariot marks more deeply the abjectness of the captive following.

Dido and Æneas—Guillaume Rouillé, *Promptuarii iconum* (1553)

And with our sprightly port make the ghosts gaze.
Dido and her Æneas shall want troops,
And all the haunt be ours.—Come, Eros, Eros!

Enter Eros.

Eros. What would my lord?
Ant. Since Cleopatra died
I have lived in such dishonor that the gods
Detest my baseness. I, that with my sword
Quartered the world and o'er green Neptune's back
With ships made cities, condemn myself to lack
The courage of a woman—less noble mind
Than she which by her death our Cæsar tells
"I am conqueror of myself." Thou art sworn, Eros,
That, when the exigent should come (which now
Is come indeed) when I should see behind me
The inevitable prosecution of
Disgrace and horror, that, on my command,
Thou then wouldst kill me. Do't; the time is come.
Thou strikest not me; 'tis Cæsar thou defeatst.
Put color in thy cheek.
Eros. The gods withhold me!
Shall I do that which all the Parthian darts,
Though enemy, lost aim and could not?
Ant. Eros,
Wouldst thou be windowed in great Rome and see
Thy master thus with pleached arms, bending down
His corrigible neck, his face subdued
To penetrative shame, whilst the wheeled seat

104. **Wherein the worship of the whole world lies:** which all the world reverences.

120-21. **got upon me/A nobleness in record:** outdone me in recording their nobility for posterity.

Of fortunate Cæsar, drawn before him, branded
His baseness that ensued?
Eros. I would not see't.
Ant. Come then; for with a wound I must be cured.
Draw that thy honest sword, which thou hast worn
Most useful for thy country.
Eros. O sir, pardon me!
Ant. When I did make thee free, sworest thou not then
To do this when I bade thee? Do it at once,
Or thy precedent services are all
But accidents unpurposed. Draw, and come.
Eros. Turn from me then that noble countenance
Wherein the worship of the whole world lies.
Ant. Lo thee! [*Turns from him.*]
Eros. My sword is drawn.
Ant. Then let it do at once
The thing why thou hast drawn it.
Eros. My dear master,
My captain, and my emperor, let me say,
Before I strike this bloody stroke, farewell.
Ant. 'Tis said, man; and farewell.
Eros. Farewell, great chief. Shall I strike now?
Ant. Now, Eros.
Eros. Why, there then! Thus I do escape the sorrow
Of Antony's death. *Kills himself.*
Ant. Thrice nobler than myself!
Thou teachest me, O valiant Eros, what
I should, and thou couldst not. My queen and Eros
Have by their brave instruction got upon me
A nobleness in record. But I will be

Ent. after l. 126. **Guard:** a body of guards.

132. **his period:** its end.

140. **enter me with:** "get me in with"; put me in the favor of.

A bridegroom in my death and run into't
As to a lover's bed. Come then; and, Eros,
Thy master dies thy scholar. To do thus
[*Falls on his sword.*]
I learned of thee. How? not dead? not dead?—
The guard, ho! O, dispatch me!

Enter [Dercetas and] a Guard.

1. Guard. What's the noise?
Ant. I have done my work ill, friends. O, make an end
Of what I have begun.
2. Guard. The star is fall'n.
1. Guard. And time is at his period.
All. Alas, and woe!
Ant. Let him that loves me strike me dead.
1. Guard. Not I.
2. Guard. Nor I.
3. Guard. Nor anyone. *Exeunt* [*Guard*].
Der. Thy death and fortunes bid thy followers fly.
This sword but shown to Cæsar, with this tidings,
Shall enter me with him.

Enter Diomedes.

Dio. Where's Antony?
Der. There, Diomed, there.
Dio. Lives he?
Wilt thou not answer, man?
[*Exit Dercetas.*]

156. **found:** adjudged true on examination of the facts.

157. **disposed:** composed, agreed.

158. **purged:** expelled, cleared out.

Ant. Art thou there, Diomed? Draw thy sword and give me
Sufficing strokes for death.
Dio. Most absolute lord,
My mistress Cleopatra sent me to thee.
Ant. When did she send thee?
Dio. Now, my lord.
Ant. Where is she?
Dio. Locked in her monument. She had a prophesying fear
Of what hath come to pass; for when she saw
(Which never shall be found) you did suspect
She had disposed with Cæsar, and that your rage
Would not be purged, she sent you word she was dead;
But, fearing since how it might work, hath sent
Me to proclaim the truth; and I am come,
I dread, too late.
Ant. Too late, good Diomed. Call my guard, I prithee.
Dio. What ho! the Emperor's guard! the guard, what ho!
Come, your lord calls!

Enter four or five of the Guard of Antony.

Ant. Bear me, good friends, where Cleopatra bides.
'Tis the last service that I shall command you.
1. Guard. Woe, woe are we, sir, you may not live to wear
All your true followers out.

173. **heavy:** sorrowful.
175. **To grace:** by honoring.

[IV. xv.] Ent. **aloft:** presumably on the upper stage.

All. Most heavy day!
Ant. Nay, good my fellows, do not please sharp fate
To grace it with your sorrows. Bid that welcome
Which comes to punish us, and we punish it,
Seeming to bear it lightly. Take me up.
I have led you oft; carry me now, good friends,
And have my thanks for all.
Exeunt, bearing Antony.

[Scene XV. Alexandria. A monument.]

Enter Cleopatra and her Maids aloft, with Charmian and Iras.

Cleo. O Charmian, I will never go from hence.
Char. Be comforted, dear madam.
Cleo. No, I will not.
All strange and terrible events are welcome,
But comforts we despise. Our size of sorrow,
Proportioned to our cause, must be as great
As that which makes it.

Enter Diomed [below].

How now? Is he dead?
Dio. His death's upon him, but not dead.
Look out o' the other side your monument.
His guard have brought him thither.

13. **Darkling:** in darkness.

23. **importune:** that is, beg for delay.

30. **brooched:** ornamented.

33. **still conclusion:** calm and quiet condemnation.

34. **Demuring upon:** presumably, looking demurely upon. Cleopatra feels that Octavia's quiet modesty will be a silent reproach to her own more flamboyant personality.

38. **Here's sport indeed:** an ironic allusion to happier times.

Enter, [below,] Antony and the Guard [bearing him].

Cleo. O sun,
Burn the great sphere thou movest in! Darkling stand
The varying shore o' the world! O Antony,
Antony, Antony! Help, Charmian; help, Iras; help!
Help, friends below! Let's draw him hither.

Ant. Peace!
Not Cæsar's valor hath o'erthrown Antony,
But Antony's hath triumphed on itself.

Cleo. So it should be, that none but Antony
Should conquer Antony; but woe 'tis so!

Ant. I am dying, Egypt, dying; only
I here importune death awhile, until
Of many thousand kisses the poor last
I lay upon thy lips.

Cleo. I dare not, dear.
Dear my lord, pardon! I dare not,
Lest I be taken. Not the imperious show
Of the full-fortuned Cæsar ever shall
Be brooched with me! If knife, drugs, serpents have
Edge, sting, or operation, I am safe.
Your wife Octavia, with her modest eyes
And still conclusion, shall acquire no honor
Demuring upon me. But come, come, Antony!
Help me, my women. We must draw thee up.
Assist, good friends.

Ant. O, quick, or I am gone.

Cleo. Here's sport indeed! How heavy weighs my lord!

40. **heaviness:** sorrow.

46. **Quicken:** revive, as at I. [iii.] 87.

51. **rail so high:** scold so forcefully.

52. **huswife:** hussy, wanton; see note at I. [ii.] 141.

Guillaume Du Choul, *Discours de la religion des anciens Romains* (1556)

Our strength is all gone into heaviness:
That makes the weight. Had I great Juno's power,
The strong-winged Mercury should fetch thee up
And set thee by Jove's side. Yet come a little!
Wishers were ever fools. O, come, come, come!

They heave Antony aloft to Cleopatra.

And welcome, welcome! Die where thou hast lived!
Quicken with kissing. Had my lips that power,
Thus would I wear them out.

All. A heavy sight!

Ant. I am dying, Egypt, dying.
Give me some wine, and let me speak a little.

Cleo. No, let me speak; and let me rail so high
That the false huswife Fortune break her wheel,
Provoked by my offense.

Ant. One word, sweet queen.
Of Cæsar seek your honor, with your safety. O!

Cleo. They do not go together.

Ant. Gentle, hear me.
None about Cæsar trust but Proculeius.

Cleo. My resolution and my hands I'll trust;
None about Cæsar.

Ant. The miserable change now at my end
Lament nor sorrow at; but please your thoughts
In feeding them with those my former fortunes,
Wherein I lived the greatest prince o' the world,
The noblest; and do now not basely die,
Not cowardly put off my helmet to
My countryman—a Roman by a Roman
Valiantly vanquished. Now my spirit is going.
I can no more.

75-6. **withered is the garland of the war,/The soldier's pole is fall'n:** that is, there can be no more rejoicing at military victory—the greatest soldier of the world is gone.

77. **odds:** points of difference. By Antony's death all the world has been leveled to mediocrity.

79. **visiting moon:** a reference to the regular return of the moon in its various phases.

88. **No more but e'en a woman:** nothing but a woman (no empress).

89. **passion:** grief.

90. **chares:** chores.

94. **Patience is sottish:** calm endurance is stupid.

Cleo. Noblest of men, woo't die?
Hast thou no care of me? Shall I abide
In this dull world, which in thy absence is
No better than a sty? O, see, my women,
[*Antony dies.*]
The crown o' the earth doth melt. My lord!
O, withered is the garland of the war,
The soldier's pole is fall'n! Young boys and girls
Are level now with men. The odds is gone,
And there is nothing left remarkable
Beneath the visiting moon. [*Swoons.*]

Char. O quietness; lady!

Iras. She's dead too, our sovereign.

Char. Lady!

Iras. Madam!

Char. O madam, madam, madam!

Iras. Royal Egypt!
Empress!

Char. Peace, peace, Iras!

Cleo. No more but e'en a woman, and commanded
By such poor passion as the maid that milks
And does the meanest chares. It were for me
To throw my scepter at the injurious gods,
To tell them that this world did equal theirs
Till they had stol'n our jewel. All's but naught.
Patience is sottish, and impatience does
Become a dog that's mad. Then is it sin
To rush into the secret house of death
Ere death dare come to us? How do you, women?
What, what! good cheer! Why, how now, Charmian?
My noble girls! Ah, women, women, look!

Our lamp is spent, it's out! Good sirs, take heart.
We'll bury him; and then, what's brave, what's noble,
Let's do it after the high Roman fashion
And make death proud to take us. Come, away!
This case of that huge spirit now is cold.
Ah, women, women! Come; we have no friend
But resolution and the briefest end.

Exeunt; [those above] bearing off Antony's body.

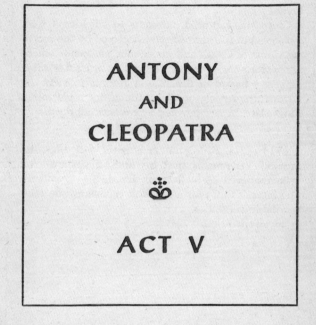

ANTONY AND CLEOPATRA

ACT V

[V.] Dercetas, who had witnessed Antony's self-wounding, takes the sword and the news to Cæsar, who sends Proculeius to give Cleopatra promises of merciful treatment. He contemplates the splendor that the Egyptian Queen will add to his triumph in Rome.

Cleopatra, captured, attempts to kill herself with a dagger but is disarmed. Not deceived by the soothing words of Cæsar and his envoys, she sends one of her women for a country fellow to bring her some asps in a basket of figs. Cæsar returns to view the sorrowful spectacle of Cleopatra in her royal robes, surrounded by her devoted attendants, all dead.

[V. i.] 2-3. **Being so frustrate, tell him, he mocks/The pauses that he makes:** since he has been rendered so ineffectual, his delays in submitting himself to Cæsar are hollow mockeries—he must inevitably surrender.

20. **civil:** urban.

[*ACT V*]

[Scene I. Alexandria. Cæsar's camp.]

Enter Cæsar, Agrippa, Dolabella, Mæcenas, [*Gallus, Proculeius, and others*], *his Council of War.*

Cæs. Go to him, Dolabella; bid him yield.
Being so frustrate, tell him, he mocks
The pause that he makes.
Dol. Cæsar, I shall. [*Exit*]

Enter Dercetas, with the sword of Antony.

Cæs. Wherefore is that? And what art thou that darest
Appear thus to us?
Der. I am called Dercetas.
Mark Antony I served, who best was worthy
Best to be served. Whilst he stood up and spoke,
He was my master, and I wore my life
To spend upon his haters. If thou please
To take me to thee, as I was to him
I'll be to Cæsar; if thou pleasest not,
I yield thee up my life.
Cæs. What is't thou sayst?
Der. I say, O Cæsar, Antony is dead.
Cæs. The breaking of so great a thing should make
A greater crack. The round world
Should have shook lions into civil streets
And citizens to their dens. The death of Antony

23. **moiety:** half.

26. **self:** same.

37. **persisted deeds:** deeds achieved by long persistence.

39. **Waged equal with him:** were proportioned equally in him.

41. **humanity:** any man.

46. **lanch:** lance, to disperse the poison of infection.

47-9. **I must perforce/Have shown to thee such a declining day/Or look on thine:** it was inevitable that one of us would witness the other's destruction; **stall:** dwell.

51. **sovereign:** overwhelming.

Is not a single doom; in the name lay
A moiety of the world.
Der. He is dead, Cæsar,
Not by a public minister of justice
Nor by a hired knife; but that self hand
Which writ his honor in the acts it did
Hath, with the courage which the heart did lend it,
Splitted the heart. This is his sword.
I robbed his wound of it. Behold it stained
With his most noble blood.
Cæs. Look you sad, friends?
The gods rebuke me but it is tidings
To wash the eyes of kings!
Agr. And strange it is
That nature must compel us to lament
Our most persisted deeds.
Mæc. His taints and honors
Waged equal with him.
Agr. A rarer spirit never
Did steer humanity; but you gods will give us
Some faults to make us men. Cæsar is touched.
Mæc. When such a spacious mirror's set before him,
He needs must see himself.
Cæs. O Antony,
I have followed thee to this! But we do lanch
Diseases in our bodies. I must perforce
Have shown to thee such a declining day
Or look on thine: we could not stall together
In the whole world. But yet let me lament
With tears as sovereign as the blood of hearts

52. **competitor:** colleague, as before at I. [iv.] 3 and [II. vii.] 86-7.

53. **In top of all design:** in enterprises of the greatest importance.

56. **Where mine his thoughts did kindle:** i.e., where my own heart found its inspiration.

57-8. **divide/Our equalness to this:** cause so great a cleavage between two who had been equal partners.

59. **meeter:** more appropriate.

71. **live:** Rowe's reading for the Folio "leave."

76. **passion:** grief, as at [IV. xv.] 89.

78-9. **her life in Rome/Would be eternal in our triumph:** i.e., her living presence in Rome at my triumph would be ever remembered.

That thou, my brother, my competitor
In top of all design, my mate in empire,
Friend and companion in the front of war,
The arm of mine own body, and the heart
Where mine his thoughts did kindle—that our stars,
Unreconciliable, should divide
Our equalness to this. Hear me, good friends—

Enter an Egyptian.

But I will tell you at some meeter season.
The business of this man looks out of him;
We'll hear him what he says. Whence are you?
Egyp. A poor Egyptian yet. The Queen my mistress,
Confined in all she has, her monument,
Of thy intents desires instruction,
That she preparedly may frame herself
To the way she's forced to.
Cæs. Bid her have good heart.
She soon shall know of us, by some of ours,
How honorable and how kindly we
Determine for her; for Cæsar cannot live
To be ungentle.
Egyp. So the gods preserve thee! *Exit.*
Cæs. Come hither, Proculeius. Go and say
We purpose her no shame. Give her what comforts
The quality of her passion shall require,
Lest, in her greatness, by some mortal stroke
She do defeat us; for her life in Rome

[V. ii.] 1-2. **My desolation does begin to make/ A better life:** i.e., since worldly fortune has left her, Cleopatra determines that her conduct will henceforth show nobility of spirit.

3. **knave:** menial.

6. **shackles accidents and bolts up change:** i.e., prevents anything further from happening.

7-8. **palates:** tastes; **dung,/The beggar's nurse and Caesar's:** earth, from which Cæsar no less than the common run of mankind receives his nourishment.

Would be eternal in our triumph. Go,
And with your speediest bring us what she says
And how you find of her.

Pro. Cæsar, I shall. *Exit.*

Cæs. Gallus, go you along. [*Exit Gallus.*] Where's Dolabella,
To second Proculeius?

All. Dolabella!

Cæs. Let him alone, for I remember now
How he's employed. He shall in time be ready.
Go with me to my tent; where you shall see
How hardly I was drawn into this war,
How calm and gentle I proceeded still
In all my writings. Go with me and see
What I can show in this.

Exeunt.

[Scene II. Alexandria. The monument.]

Enter Cleopatra, Charmian, Iras, and Mardian.

Cleo. My desolation does begin to make
A better life. 'Tis paltry to be Cæsar.
Not being Fortune, he's but Fortune's knave,
A minister of her will. And it is great
To do that thing that ends all other deeds,
Which shackles accidents and bolts up change,
Which sleeps, and never palates more the dung,
The beggar's nurse and Cæsar's.

16-7. **I do not greatly care to be deceived,/ That have no use for trusting:** it makes no difference to me whether I am deceived, since I have no plans that require trustworthy friends.

19. **keep decorum:** behave properly; see I. [ii.] 76.

22. **as:** that.

26. **Make your full reference freely:** entrust yourself fully and unreservedly.

29. **sweet dependency:** agreeable submission.

30. **pray in aid for kindness:** ask you to assist his kindness; i.e., to assist him in being kind to you. **Pray in aid** is a legal term meaning to crave assistance.

33-4. **send him/The greatness he has got:** acknowledge that he is my conqueror.

Enter Proculeius.

Pro. Cæsar sends greeting to the Queen of Egypt,
And bids thee study on what fair demands
Thou meanst to have him grant thee.

Cleo. What's thy name?

Pro. My name is Proculeius.

Cleo. Antony
Did tell me of you, bade me trust you; but
I do not greatly care to be deceived,
That have no use for trusting. If your master
Would have a queen his beggar, you must tell him
That majesty, to keep decorum, must
No less beg than a kingdom. If he please
To give me conquered Egypt for my son,
He gives me so much of mine own as I
Will kneel to him with thanks.

Pro. Be of good cheer.
Y'are fall'n into a princely hand; fear nothing.
Make your full reference freely to my lord,
Who is so full of grace that it flows over
On all that need. Let me report to him
Your sweet dependency, and you shall find
A conqueror that will pray in aid for kindness,
Where he for grace is kneeled to.

Cleo. Pray you tell him
I am his fortune's vassal and I send him
The greatness he has got. I hourly learn
A doctrine of obedience, and would gladly
Look him i' the face.

40. **surprised:** captured. At this line many editors add a stage direction indicating that Proculeius and guards ascend the monument by a ladder and enter a window behind Cleopatra. Plutarch so describes the manner of Cleopatra's capture by Cæsar's men. But we feel, in common with a few other modern editors (M. R. Ridley, for example,) that this will not do. The scene must occur inside the monument, to which Proculeius might have been admitted by Cleopatra's orders, and the guards could ascend and enter a window in another room of the monument out of the audience's view.

48-9. **of death too,/That rids our dogs of languish:** that is, relieved (deprived) of the ease which death would bring.

54. **come forth:** become apparent.

58. **temperance:** calm yourself.

60. **If idle talk will once be necessary:** needless to say.

Pro. This I'll report, dear lady.
Have comfort, for I know your plight is pitied
Of him that caused it.

[*Enter Gallus and Soldiers.*]

Gal. You see how easily she may be surprised.
Guard her till Cæsar come. [*Exit.*]
Iras. Royal Queen!
Char. O Cleopatra! thou art taken, Queen!
Cleo. Quick, quick, good hands! [*Draws a dagger.*]
Pro. Hold, worthy lady, hold!
[*Disarms her.*]
Do not yourself such wrong, who are in this
Relieved, but not betrayed.
Cleo. What, of death too,
That rids our dogs of languish?
Pro. Cleopatra,
Do not abuse my master's bounty by
The undoing of yourself. Let the world see
His nobleness well acted, which your death
Will never let come forth.
Cleo. Where art thou, death?
Come hither, come! Come, come, and take a queen
Worth many babes and beggars!
Pro. O, temperance, lady!
Cleo. Sir, I will eat no meat; I'll not drink, sir;
If idle talk will once be necessary,
I'll not sleep neither. This mortal house I'll ruin,
Do Cæsar what he can. Know, sir, that I
Will not wait pinioned at your master's court

66. **varletry:** group of menials, hence, rabble.

70. **Blow me into abhorring:** make an abhorrent thing of me by swelling my dead body with their eggs.

71. **pyramides:** pyramids.

78. **For:** as for.

An Egyptian pyramid—André Thevet, *Cosmographie de Levant* (1554)

Nor once be chastised with the sober eye
Of dull Octavia. Shall they hoist me up
And show me to the shouting varletry
Of censuring Rome? Rather a ditch in Egypt
Be gentle grave unto me! Rather on Nilus' mud
Lay me stark-naked and let the waterflies
Blow me into abhorring! Rather make
My country's high pyramides my gibbet
And hang me up in chains!

Pro. You do extend
These thoughts of horror further than you shall
Find cause in Cæsar.

Enter Dolabella.

Dol. Proculeius,
What thou hast done thy master Cæsar knows,
And he hath sent me for thee. For the Queen,
I'll take her to my guard.

Pro. So, Dolabella,
It shall content me best. Be gentle to her.
[*To Cleopatra*] To Cæsar I will speak what you shall
please,
If you'll employ me to him.

Cleo. Say, I would die.

Exeunt Proculeius [and Soldiers].

Dol. Most noble Empress, you have heard of me?

Cleo. I cannot tell.

Dol. Assuredly you know me.

Cleo. No matter, sir, what I have heard or known.

91. **trick:** habit.

101-2. **his reared arm/Crested the world:** his might dominated the world. The word **crested** was apparently suggested by the idea of a heraldic crest, many of which portray a raised arm in a threatening posture.

102-3. **was propertied/As all the tuned spheres:** i.e., was as harmonious as the music of the spheres. Cf. *Merchant of Venice,* V. i. 68-70: "There's not the smallest orb which thou beholdst/ But in his motion like an angel sings,/Still quiring to the young-eyed cherubins."

104. **quail and shake:** cause to quail and shake, terrify; **orb:** globe; i.e., the earth.

106-7. **an autumn 'twas/That grew the more by reaping:** that is, like the fruits of an abundant harvest, his bounty seemed inexhaustible. Theobald read **autumn** for the Folio "Anthony."

107-9. **His delights/Were dolphin-like: they showed his back above/The element they lived in:** Antony, in his delights, was dolphin-like; like a porpoise he always rode above the tide of his pleasures.

109-10. **In his livery/Walked crowns and crownets:** that is, he was attended by the wearers of crowns and coronets—kings and peers.

112. **plates:** silver coins, a name derived from the Spanish coin *real de plata.*

119. **wants:** lacks.

You laugh when boys or women tell their dreams;
Is't not your trick?
Dol. I understand not, madam.
Cleo. I dreamt there was an Emperor Antony—
O, such another sleep, that I might see
But such another man!
Dol. If it might please ye—
Cleo. His face was as the heav'ns, and therein stuck
A sun and moon, which kept their course and lighted
The little O, the earth.
Dol. Most sovereign creature—
Cleo. His legs bestrid the ocean: his reared arm
Crested the world. His voice was propertied
As all the tuned spheres, and that to friends;
But when he meant to quail and shake the orb,
He was as rattling thunder. For his bounty,
There was no winter in't; an autumn 'twas
That grew the more by reaping. His delights
Were dolphin-like: they showed his back above
The element they lived in. In his livery
Walked crowns and crownets. Realms and islands were
As plates dropped from his pocket.
Dol. Cleopatra—
Cleo. Think you there was or might be such a man
As this I dreamt of?
Dol. Gentle madam, no.
Cleo. You lie, up to the hearing of the gods!
But, if there be or ever were one such,
It's past the size of dreaming. Nature wants stuff

120-22. **vie strange forms with fancy:** compete with fancy in the creation of remarkable forms; **t'imagine/An Antony were nature's piece 'gainst fancy,/Condemning shadows quite:** when we re-create an Antony in our imagination we have a genuine masterpiece of nature that quite puts to shame the shadowy creations of fancy.

126. **but I do:** if I do not.

To vie strange forms with fancy; yet, t'imagine
An Antony were nature's piece 'gainst fancy,
Condemning shadows quite.
Dol. Hear me, good madam.
Your loss is as yourself, great; and you bear it
As answering to the weight. Would I might never
O'ertake pursued success but I do feel,
By the rebound of yours, a grief that smites
My very heart at root.
Cleo. I thank you, sir.
Know you what Cæsar means to do with me?
Dol. I am loath to tell you what I would you knew.
Cleo. Nay, pray you, sir.
Dol. Though he be honorable—
Cleo. He'll lead me, then, in triumph?
Dol. Madam, he will. I know't. *Flourish.*
[*Shout within.*] "Make way there! Cæsar!"

Enter Proculeius; Cæsar [*with*] *Gallus, Mæcenas, and others of his Train,* [*Seleucus following*].

Cæs. Which is the Queen of Egypt?
Dol. It is the Emperor, madam.
Cleopatra kneels.
Cæs. Arise! You shall not kneel.
I pray you rise. Rise, Egypt.
Cleo. Sir, the gods
Will have it thus. My master and my lord
I must obey.
Cæs. Take to you no hard thoughts.
The record of what injuries you did us,

149. **project:** set forth.

150. **clear:** blameless.

154. **extenuate rather than enforce:** excuse rather than emphasize (your faults).

155. **apply:** submit.

163. **may, through all the world:** i.e., there is no part of the world where he is not free to come and go as he wishes.

165. **scutcheons:** literally, shields bearing coats of arms; therefore, symbols of greatness.

168. **brief:** list.

170. **Not petty things admitted:** not including trivial items.

Though written in our flesh, we shall remember
As things but done by chance.
Cleo. Sole sir o' the world,
I cannot project mine own cause so well
To make it clear, but do confess I have
Been laden with like frailties which before
Have often shamed our sex.
Cæs. Cleopatra, know
We will extenuate rather than enforce.
If you apply yourself to our intents,
Which towards you are most gentle, you shall find
A benefit in this change; but if you seek
To lay on me a cruelty by taking
Antony's course, you shall bereave yourself
Of my good purposes, and put your children
To that destruction which I'll guard them from
If thereon you rely. I'll take my leave.
Cleo. And may, through all the world! 'Tis yours, and we,
Your scutcheons and your signs of conquest, shall
Hang in what place you please. Here, my good lord.
Cæs. You shall advise me in all for Cleopatra.
Cleo. This is the brief of money, plate, and jewels
I am possessed of. 'Tis exactly valued,
Not petty things admitted. Where's Seleucus?
Sel. Here, madam.
Cleo. This is my treasurer. Let him speak, my lord,
Upon his peril, that I have reserved
To myself nothing. Speak the truth, Seleucus.
Sel. Madam,

176. **seel:** sew up, as at [III. xiii.] 139.

184. **How pomp is followed:** how faithfully the great are served.

185. **estates:** conditions.

198-99. **Parcel the sum of my disgraces by/ Addition of his envy:** i.e., by his malicious conduct add another misfortune to the many I have already experienced.

201. **Immoment toys:** inconsequential trifles; **dignity:** value, estimation.

202. **modern:** ordinary.

204. **Livia:** the wife of Octavius Cæsar.

205-6. **unfolded/With:** exposed by.

Livia–Jacobus de Strada, ***Epitome thesauri antiquitatum*** **(1557)**

I had rather seel my lips than to my peril
Speak that which is not.
Cleo. What have I kept back?
Sel. Enough to purchase what you have made known.
Cæs. Nay, blush not, Cleopatra. I approve
Your wisdom in the deed.
Cleo. See, Cæsar! O, behold,
How pomp is followed! Mine will now be yours;
And should we shift estates, yours would be mine.
The ingratitude of this Seleucus does
Even make me wild. O slave, of no more trust
Than love that's hired! What, goest thou back? Thou shalt
Go back, I warrant thee; but I'll catch thine eyes,
Though they had wings. Slave, soulless villain, dog!
O rarely base!
Cæs. Good Queen, let us entreat you.
Cleo. O Cæsar, what a wounding shame is this,
That thou vouchsafing here to visit me,
Doing the honor of thy lordliness
To one so meek, that mine own servant should
Parcel the sum of my disgraces by
Addition of his envy! Say, good Cæsar,
That I some lady trifles have reserved,
Immoment toys, things of such dignity
As we greet modern friends withal; and say
Some nobler token I have kept apart
For Livia and Octavia, to induce
Their mediation—must I be unfolded
With one that I have bred? The gods! It smites me

209-10. **show the cinders of my spirits/ Through the ashes of my chance:** display some of the fire of my former queenly temper, despite the fact that my good fortune is almost burned out.

212. **Forbear:** leave us, as at I. [ii.] 137.

213-16. **we, the greatest, are misthought/For things that others do; and, when we fall,/We answer others' merits in our name:** we great ones are misjudged because of the deeds of our subordinates, and, when we fall, we suffer in our own persons the deserts of others.

222. **make prize:** bargain.

Beneath the fall I have. [*To Seleucus*] Prithee go hence!
Or I shall show the cinders of my spirits
Through the ashes of my chance. Wert thou a man,
Thou wouldst have mercy on me.

Cæs. Forbear, Seleucus.

[*Exit Seleucus.*]

Cleo. Be it known that we, the greatest, are misthought
For things that others do; and, when we fall,
We answer others' merits in our name,
Are therefore to be pitied.

Cæs. Cleopatra,
Not what you have reserved, nor what acknowledged,
Put we i' the roll of conquest. Still be't yours,
Bestow it at your pleasure; and believe
Cæsar's no merchant, to make prize with you
Of things that merchants sold. Therefore be cheered;
Make not your thoughts your prisons. No, dear Queen;
For we intend so to dispose you as
Yourself shall give us counsel. Feed and sleep.
Our care and pity is so much upon you
That we remain your friend; and so adieu.

Cleo. My master and my lord!

Cæs. Not so. Adieu.

Flourish. Exeunt Cæsar and his Train.

Cleo. He words me, girls, he words me, that I should not
Be noble to myself! But hark thee, Charmian.

[*Whispers to Charmian.*]

257. **puppet:** contemptuous term for a woman.

258. **Mechanic slaves:** base working men; see **mechanic** at [IV. iv.] 42 note.

261. **Rank of:** smelling offensive because of.

Iras. Finish, good lady. The bright day is done,
And we are for the dark.
Cleo. Hie thee again.
I have spoke already, and it is provided.
Go put it to the haste.
Char. Madam, I will.

[*Re-*]*enter Dolabella.*

Dol. Where is the Queen?
Char. Behold, sir. [*Exit.*]
Cleo. Dolabella!
Dol. Madam, as thereto sworn, by your command
(Which my love makes religion to obey)
I tell you this: Cæsar through Syria
Intends his journey, and within three days
You with your children will he send before.
Make your best use of this. I have performed
Your pleasure and my promise.
Cleo. Dolabella,
I shall remain your debtor.
Dol. I your servant.
Adieu, good Queen; I must attend on Cæsar.
Cleo. Farewell, and thanks. *Exit* [*Dolabella*].
Now, Iras, what thinkst thou?
Thou, an Egyptian puppet, shall be shown
In Rome as well as I. Mechanic slaves,
With greasy aprons, rules, and hammers, shall
Uplift us to the view. In their thick breaths,
Rank of gross diet, shall we be enclouded,
And forced to drink their vapor.

264. **lictors:** officials of the Roman state who attended on magistrates and were usually of low birth. H. H. Furness is probably correct in suggesting that Shakespeare equates **lictors** with the Elizabethan beadles, who among their other duties saw to the correction of whores.

265. **scald:** scurvy, contemptible.

266. **Ballad us:** write popular ballads about us. The less talented writers of Elizabethan London were quick to write ballads about any contemporary event that was lurid or pathetic, and these were often printed on single sheets and sold in the streets; **quick:** inventive; **comedians:** actors.

270. **boy:** a reference to the contemporary practice of having all feminine roles played by immature boys. No women appeared on the English stage until after 1660.

271. **posture:** conduct.

282. **Sirrah:** a familiar term of address to both men and women.

Iras. The gods forbid!
Cleo. Nay, 'tis most certain, Iras. Saucy lictors
Will catch at us like strumpets, and scald rhymers
Ballad us out o' tune. The quick comedians
Extemporally will stage us and present
Our Alexandrian revels. Antony
Shall be brought drunken forth, and I shall see
Some squeaking Cleopatra boy my greatness
I' the posture of a whore.
Iras. O the good gods!
Cleo. Nay, that's certain.
Iras. I'll never see't; for I am sure my nails
Are stronger than mine eyes.
Cleo. Why, that's the way
To fool their preparation and to conquer
Their most absurd intents.

[*Re-*]*enter Charmian.*

Now, Charmian!
Show me, my women, like a queen. Go fetch
My best attires. I am again for Cydnus,
To meet Mark Antony. Sirrah Iras, go.
Now, noble Charmian, we'll dispatch indeed;
And when thou hast done this chare, I'll give thee leave
To play till doomsday.—Bring our crown and all.
[*Exit Iras.*]
A noise within.
Wherefore's this noise?

292. **What:** how.

294. **placed:** firmly set.

296. **fleeting moon:** i.e., the "inconstant moon" as in *Romeo and Juliet,* [II. ii.] 114. Cleopatra refers to her identification with Isis.

Ent. after l. 297. **Clown:** an epithet for a country fellow as well as for a comic.

299. **Avoid:** withdraw.

306. **on't:** of it.

308. **honest:** a quibble. The word meant "chaste" and "honorable" as well as being used in the more general modern sense.

Enter a Guardsman.

Guard. Here is a rural fellow
That will not be denied your Highness' presence.
He brings you figs.

Cleo. Let him come in. *Exit Guardsman.*
What poor an instrument
May do a noble deed! He brings me liberty.
My resolution's placed, and I have nothing
Of woman in me. Now from head to foot
I am marble-constant. Now the fleeting moon
No planet is of mine.

Enter Guardsman and Clown [with basket].

Guard. This is the man.

Cleo. Avoid, and leave him. *Exit Guardsman.*
Hast thou the pretty worm of Nilus there
That kills and pains not?

Clown. Truly I have him. But I would not be the party that should desire you to touch him, for his biting is immortal. Those that do die of it do seldom or never recover.

Cleo. Rememberst thou any that have died on't?

Clown. Very many, men and women too. I heard of one of them no longer than yesterday—a very honest woman, but something given to lie, as a woman should not do but in the way of honesty—how she died of the biting of it, what pain she felt. Truly, she makes a very good report o' the worm; but he that

314. **falliable:** infallible, certain.

320. **do his kind:** act according to his nature.

332. **dress:** prepare.

332. **whoreson:** a jocular epithet not meant literally.

338. **Immortal longings:** longings for death.

will believe all that they say shall never be saved by half that they do. But this is most falliable, the worm's an odd worm.

Cleo. Get thee hence; farewell.

Clown. I wish you all joy of the worm.

[*Sets down his basket.*]

Cleo. Farewell.

Clown. You must think this, look you, that the worm will do his kind.

Cleo. Ay, ay; farewell.

Clown. Look you, the worm is not to be trusted but in the keeping of wise people, for indeed there is no goodness in the worm.

Cleo. Take thou no care; it shall be heeded.

Clown. Very good. Give it nothing, I pray you, for it is not worth the feeding.

Cleo. Will it eat me?

Clown. You must not think I am so simple but I know the Devil himself will not eat a woman. I know that a woman is a dish for the gods, if the Devil dress her not. But truly, these same whoreson devils do the gods great harm in their women; for in every ten that they make, the devils mar five.

Cleo. Well, get thee gone; farewell.

Clown. Yes, forsooth. I wish you joy o' the worm.

Exit.

[*Enter Iras with a robe, crown, etc.*]

Cleo. Give me my robe, put on my crown. I have
Immortal longings in me. Now no more
The juice of Egypt's grape shall moist this lip.

340. **Yare:** be quick and deft; see [III. vii.] 49 and [III. xiii.] 160.

345. **title:** right.

346. **elements:** see note for [II. vii.] 50.

350. **aspic:** a variant form of "asp."

358. **This proves me base:** that is, Iras' death proves Cleopatra base in that she herself still lives.

361. **mortal:** deadly.

363. **intrinsicate:** intricate, a word apparently derived from the Latin *intrinsecato* by confusing it with *intricato*.

367. **Unpolicied:** wanting in cunning or statesmanship.

An asp of the Nile—Pierre Belon, *Observations de plusieurs singularitez* (1588)

Yare, yare, good Iras; quick. Methinks I hear
Antony call. I see him rouse himself
To praise my noble act. I hear him mock
The luck of Cæsar, which the gods give men
To excuse their after wrath. Husband, I come!
Now to that name my courage prove my title!
I am fire and air; my other elements
I give to baser life. So, have you done?
Come then and take the last warmth of my lips.
Farewell, kind Charmian. Iras, long farewell.
[*Kisses them. Iras falls and dies.*]
Have I the aspic in my lips? Dost fall?
If thou and nature can so gently part,
The stroke of death is as a lover's pinch,
Which hurts, and is desired. Dost thou lie still?
If thus thou vanishest, thou tellst the world
It is not worth leave-taking.

Char. Dissolve, thick cloud, and rain, that I may say
The gods themselves do weep!

Cleo. This proves me base.
If she first meet the curled Antony,
He'll make demand of her, and spend that kiss
Which is my heaven to have. Come, thou mortal wretch,
[*To an asp, which she applies to her breast.*]
With thy sharp teeth this knot intrinsicate
Of life at once untie. Poor venomous fool,
Be angry, and dispatch. O, couldst thou speak,
That I might hear thee call great Cæsar ass
Unpolicied!

Char. O Eastern star!

376. **vile:** Capell's reading for the Folio "wilde."

Phœbus—Vincenzo Cartari, *Imagini de gli dei delli antichi* (1615)

Cleo. Peace, peace!
Dost thou not see my baby at my breast,
That sucks the nurse asleep?
Char. O, break! O, break!
Cleo. As sweet as balm, as soft as air, as gentle—
O Antony! Nay, I will take thee too:
[*Applies another asp to her arm.*]
What should I stay— *Dies.*
Char. In this vile world? So fare thee well.
Now boast thee, death, in thy possession lies
A lass unparalleled. Downy windows, close;
And golden Phoebus never be beheld
Of eyes again so royal! Your crown's awry.
I'll mend it, and then play—

Enter the Guard, rustling in.

1. Guard. Where's the Queen?
Char. Speak softly, wake her not.
1. Guard. Cæsar hath sent—
Char. Too slow a messenger.
[*Applies an asp.*]
O, come apace, dispatch. I partly feel thee.
1. Guard. Approach, ho! All's not well. Cæsar's beguiled.
2. Guard. There's Dolabella sent from Cæsar. Call him.
1. Guard. What work is here! Charmian, is this well done?

398-99. **thy thoughts/Touch their effects in this:** i.e., what you imagined has happened. **Effect** is equivalent to "accomplishment."

405. **Bravest:** noblest.

406. **leveled:** guessed accurately; literally, aimed.

416. **trimming up:** putting straight.

Char. It is well done, and fitting for a princess
Descended of so many royal kings.
Ah, soldier! *Charmian dies.*

Enter Dolabella.

Dol. How goes it here?
2. *Guard.* All dead.
Dol. Cæsar, thy thoughts
Touch their effects in this. Thyself art coming
To see performed the dreaded act which thou
So soughtst to hinder.
[*Shout within.*] A way there, a way for Cæsar!

Enter Cæsar and all his Train.

Dol. O sir, you are too sure an augurer:
That you did fear is done.
Cæs. Bravest at the last!
She leveled at our purposes, and being royal,
Took her own way. The manner of their deaths?
I do not see them bleed.
Dol. Who was last with them?
1. *Guard.* A simple countryman, that brought her figs.
This was his basket.
Cæs. Poisoned, then.
1. *Guard.* O Cæsar,
This Charmian lived but now; she stood and spake.
I found her trimming up the diadem

422. **As:** as if.

423. **toil:** net, snare.

425. **something blown:** somewhat swollen.

433. **pursued conclusions infinite:** experimented infinitely.

437. **clip:** enclose, embrace, as at [IV. viii.] 8.

439. **those that make them:** i.e., those ultimately responsible for them—Cæsar, in this case.

On her dead mistress. Tremblingly she stood,
And on the sudden dropped.

Cæs. O noble weakness!
If they had swallowed poison, 'twould appear
By external swelling; but she looks like sleep,
As she would catch another Antony
In her strong toil of grace.

Dol. Here on her breast
There is a vent of blood, and something blown;
The like is on her arm.

1. Guard. This is an aspic's trail; and these fig leaves
Have slime upon them, such as the aspic leaves
Upon the caves of Nile.

Cæs. Most probable
That so she died; for her physician tells me
She hath pursued conclusions infinite
Of easy ways to die. Take up her bed,
And bear her women from the monument.
She shall be buried by her Antony.
No grave upon the earth shall clip in it
A pair so famous. High events as these
Strike those that make them; and their story is
No less in pity than his glory which
Brought them to be lamented. Our army shall
In solemn show attend this funeral,
And then to Rome. Come, Dolabella, see
High order in this great solemnity.

Exeunt omnes.

KEY TO

Famous Lines and Phrases

There's beggary in the love that can be reckoned.
[*Antony*—I. i. 16-7]

Let Rome in Tiber melt and the wide arch
Of the ranged empire fall! Here is my space.
[*Antony*—I. i. 38-9]

Who tells me true, though in his tale lie death,
I hear him as he flattered. [*Antony*—I. ii. 106-7]

Eternity was in our lips and eyes,
Bliss in our brows' bent. [*Cleopatra*—I. iii. 48-9]

My salad days,
When I was green in judgment, cold in blood.
[*Cleopatra*—I. v. 87-8]

The barge she sat in, like a burnished throne,
Burned on the water. . . . [*Enobarbus*—II. ii. 237 ff.]

Age cannot wither her nor custom stale
Her infinite variety. [*Enobarbus*—II. ii. 286-87]

Her tongue will not obey her heart, nor can
Her heart inform her tongue—the swan's-down feather
That stands upon the swell at full of tide,
And neither way inclines. [*Antony*—III. ii. 59-62]

We have kissed away kingdoms and provinces.
[*Scarus*—III. x. 10-1]

O this false soul of Egypt! this grave charm . . .
Like a right gypsy hath at fast and loose
Beguiled me to the very heart of loss! [*Antony*—IV. xii. 28-33]

Unarm, Eros. The long day's task is done,
And we must sleep. [*Antony*—IV. xiv. 45-6]

We'll bury him; and then, what's brave, what's noble,
Let's do it after the high Roman fashion
And make death proud to take us. [*Cleopatra*—IV. xv. 101-3]

Finish, good lady. The bright day is done,
And we are for the dark. [*Iras*—V. ii. 235-36]

Give me my robe, put on my crown. I have
Immortal longings in me. [*Cleopatra*—V. ii. 337-38]

She looks like sleep,
As she would catch another Antony
In her strong toil of grace. [*Cæsar*—V. ii. 421-23]